CW00656629

William Godwin

Also available:

William Godwin
A Political Life

Richard Gough Thomas

PLUTO PRESS

First published 2019 by Pluto Press
345 Archway Road, London N6 5AA

www.plutobooks.com

Copyright © Richard Gough Thomas 2019

The right of Richard Gough Thomas to be identified as the author of this work
has been asserted by him in accordance with the Copyright, Designs and Patents
Act 1988.

British Library Cataloguing in Publication Data
A catalogue record for this book is available from the British Library

ISBN   978 0 7453 3836 1   Hardback
ISBN   978 0 7453 3835 4   Paperback
ISBN   978 1 7868 0389 4   PDF eBook
ISBN   978 1 7868 0391 7   Kindle eBook
ISBN   978 1 7868 0390 0   EPUB eBook

This book is printed on paper suitable for recycling and made from fully managed
and sustained forest sources. Logging, pulping and manufacturing processes are
expected to conform to the environmental standards of the country of origin.

Typeset by Stanford DTP Services, Northampton, England

Simultaneously printed in the United Kingdom and United States of America

Contents

Series Preface

Revolutionary Lives is a series of short, critical biographies of radical figures from throughout history. The books are sympathetic but not sycophantic, and the intention is to present a balanced and, where necessary, critical evaluation of the individual's place in their political field, putting their actions and achievements in context and exploring issues raised by their lives, such as the use or rejection of violence, nationalism, or gender in political activism. While individuals are the subject of the books, their personal lives are dealt with lightly except insofar as they mesh with political concerns. The focus is on the contribution these revolutionaries made to history, an examination of how far they achieved their aims in improving the lives of the oppressed and exploited, and how they can continue to be an inspiration for many today.

Series Editors:
Sarah Irving, King's College, London
Professor Paul Le Blanc, La Roche College, Pittsburgh

Acknowledgements

My heartfelt thanks must go out to everyone involved with Newcastle University's *William Godwin: Forms, Fears, Futures* conference in 2017, and the community of Godwin scholars across the world. I am immensely grateful to Professor Mark Philp for his encouragement, and this book is stronger and richer for the suggestions and advice of John-Erik Hansen.

Thanks must also go to David Castle and Robert Webb at Pluto Press for their patience with a first-time author.

Finally, the book would never have been written without the urging of Joshua M. Reynolds, or the support of Jen Edwards, Alex Burnett and Angharad Thomas.

1

Introduction
The Anarchist

His contemporaries believed him to be the most important radical thinker of their age. William Godwin (1756–1836) was a political philosopher in the purest sense – he wrote no great revolutionary speeches, nor did he ever issue a political manifesto. As the French Revolution careened from popular uprising to government terror, and from Directory to despotism, across the Channel British radicals pressed for parliamentary reform, women's rights and greater religious freedom. Godwin went further, questioning the most basic assumptions of government itself. Many of his peers were tried or imprisoned for their activism but Godwin, a lifelong critic of violence, and undeniably a theorist rather than an agitator, endured decades of abuse in the government-backed press because no political or criminal charges could ever be found against him.

William Godwin was an anarchist. He would not have understood the term in the way we do. He regarded anarchy in its popular sense, as a synonym for chaos. He recognised it as a creative chaos, however, and argued that its principal danger was that it created the conditions that might allow new (more brutal) authority to rise in its wake. Godwin was critical of authority as a principle, not merely its implementation, and believed that our ability to reason (if developed) would eventually make laws and government unnecessary. Godwin explained his ideas in *An Enquiry Concerning Political Justice* (1793), written at the height of the French Revolution when it seemed as if the world had been pitched into the kind of creative chaos where anything was possible. *Political Justice* came to be regarded as one of the first major texts in the history of anarchist thought, exemplifying what is now (loosely) defined as 'philosophical' anarchism – the theoretical basis for anti-authoritarian principles and political action. Godwin himself was not a revolutionary.

Figure 1   Godwin described James Northcote's 1803
portrait as 'the principal memorandum of my corporal
existence that will remain after my death.'
(National Portrait Gallery, London)

A quiet man, often shy among strangers, Godwin wanted to change the
world through writing and conversation, recognising that educating
people to reason for themselves was a more certain way of making things
better than imposing better things on them.

'Anarchist' is a word that conjures up images of revolutionary action,
be it via the symbolic violence of the Black Bloc or the peaceful overthrow
of the old social order in Catalonia at the beginning of the Spanish Civil
War. Yet it also describes a wide range of anti-authoritarian political
thought, on both the left and right, united only by a common resistance
to being told what to do. The word itself has an image problem: its
literal meaning is simply to be 'without rulers' but we have been told for
centuries that, without rulers, the existing order of society would tear
itself apart. We might cynically observe that the existing order could do
with a shake-up, but few of us wish to do without order at all, and we
have been led to believe that order is maintained through the exercise of

authority – of people *giving* orders and other people following them, with consequences for stepping too far out of line (because other people can't be trusted). Many anarchists would argue that order is simply something that happens when a group of people find out how to get along, and that most of the things that authority claims to protect us from are indirectly caused by authority in the first place (e.g. theft – which is caused by inequality, which usually benefits those in power). Making statements about 'what anarchists think' is, of course, a quixotic endeavour. Anarchism is a philosophy, but one that naturally defies rigid definitions. Anarchism has ideas, and it has thinkers, and it is easier to write about 'anarchisms' (or the anarchism of a particular individual) than it is to discuss every school of thought under its umbrella.

If his contribution to anarchism were the sum of Godwin's achievement, he would be an interesting figure for historians and philosophers. He was more: a novelist, historian and children's writer of enormous influence in his own time. His extensive diaries reveal his direct connection to dozens of the most important names of his time in the fields of literature, politics, science and art (too many to do justice to in one book). Most importantly, he was the loving husband of Mary Wollstonecraft – in the view of history, easily the most important feminist writer and thinker of the eighteenth century – and the father of Mary Shelley, a novelist of immense cultural significance. Their lives are closely interlinked, but this book is an account of Godwin's life and thought, and can only tackle Wollstonecraft and her daughter where their influence is crucial to Godwin's story. Readers are referred to Janet Todd's *Mary Wollstonecraft: A Revolutionary Life* (2000) for the most authoritative version of that writer's life; biographies of Mary Shelley are numerous but Anne K. Mellor's *Mary Shelley: Her Life, Her Fiction, Her Monsters* (1989) is a standard.

Godwin's story is as much held in his writing as it is in his life, and an extended discussion of his literary and philosophical works is essential to communicating why the philosopher was such a crucial (and controversial) figure in the culture of his time. This book attempts to tell the story of Godwin's life, from his rise to radical fame in the 1790s to obscurity and bankruptcy years later, and so draws extensively on his letters and diaries (preserving his idiosyncratic spelling and sometimes cryptic abbreviations). Yet it could not adequately do so without explaining the theory of Political Justice or the ideas of *The Enquirer*, nor could it explain the philosopher's character without *Caleb Williams*, *St Leon*, or his *Memoir* of Wollstonecraft. Godwin's life was a life in letters even more than it was a life in politics – his works contributed to shaping the literary, historical and educational genres that we take for granted today – and his ideas have influenced generations of thinkers up to the present day.

2

The Minister
1756–93

William Godwin was born in 1756, the son of a Dissenting minister and the grandson of another.

'Dissenter' was the name given to those Protestants who had opposed the 1662 Act of Uniformity; the Presbyterians, Baptists and Congregationalists who refused to conform with Anglican strictures on prayer, theology and the authority of the crown over the church. Their descendants traced their lineage back to the 'Independents' of the Civil War, defended (with reservations) the memory of Cromwell, and celebrated the 1688 revolution as the first step on the road to religious and political freedom.

Dissenters were found in all walks of life but, for a variety of reasons, were well-represented among artisans and merchants of the bigger towns and cities. The Test and Corporation Acts, requiring at least occasional Anglican religious observance from public officials, excluded Dissenters from parliament and municipal office. Though a small number were willing to pay lip service to the Church of England in exchange for their own seat at the table, the majority threw whatever weight they had behind the liberal Whigs. Godwin in later life was conscious of quite how much Dissenting culture had shaped him, how much it coloured his attitudes to political and cultural developments and how it affected the way he thought.

Godwin was the seventh of thirteen children, and many of his siblings did not live to see adulthood. The philosopher remembered his father as a warm-hearted (but far from clever) man, with a tendency towards austerity and ill humour that were balanced by the vivacity of Godwin's mother.[1] Disputes within congregations – many Dissenting groups reserved the right to reject ministers they could not see eye to eye with

– saw the family move from Wisbech in Cambridgeshire (where Godwin was born) to Debenham in Suffolk, before finally settling in the small village of Guestwick in Norfolk, in 1760. Somewhere either before or after William's birth, the already busy household took on a cousin, Hannah Godwin (later Sothren), as a lodger. Hannah appears to have been the young William's most important friend in early childhood. It was Hannah that introduced the future novelist to books and, in defiance of his father's particularly strict form of Calvinism, took him to the theatre at the age of nine.

William was the only one of the surviving children that felt the call to the ministry. The elder Godwin did not encourage his son's ambitions. As a small boy, William had given sermons from atop a chair in the kitchen and terrorised a schoolmate with descriptions of his damnation. The young Godwin was clever, enthusiastic and precocious, signs that his father took as symptoms of his arrogance. At the age of eleven, William was taken from the local school at Hindolveston and sent to live as the sole pupil of the Reverend Samuel Newton in Norwich. William's new teacher was far more educated, but a far stricter Calvinist (and disciplinarian) than his father. Newton was a follower of Robert Sandeman, who (as Godwin would later write) 'after Calvin had damned ninety-nine in a hundred of mankind, has contrived a scheme for damning ninety-nine in a hundred of the followers of Calvin'.[2] The young Godwin was whipped and berated for his pride, yet he formed a bond with his tutor that would last until the ideas contained in *Political Justice* drove a wedge between them.

Even writing forty years later, Godwin's memories of Newton retained a touch of anger. He was cold, 'a very insufficient master' and 'a despot', but he shaped his pupil's religious and political opinions for many years to come.[3] In his unfinished autobiography, Godwin wrote: 'Newton was certainly my friend. His sentiments towards me were singular. He always treated me as self-conceited and arrogant: yet he had a high opinion of my talents.'[4] The two remained in correspondence into the 1790s.

At fourteen, he withdrew from Newton's tutelage and returned to the school at Hindolveston. Godwin described his time under Newton as 'more vexatious than I could well endure' but within a few months he was back with Newton again, until his teacher dismissed him at the end of 1771.[5] Godwin returned home to work as an assistant at his former school. His father died the next year and soon William's mother was organising his return to study. University was probably never considered: again, Oxford and Cambridge required adherence to the Church of England. Instead, Godwin would enrol at one of the country's many Dissenting Academies – institutions that had grown up over the course of the eighteenth century to provide an educated ministry for nonconformist congregations (in the face of legal harassment by Anglicans and Tories) but, in some cases, had developed a reputation for excellence that far surpassed that of England's ancient universities. Most students went on to a religious calling, some even with the established church (such as Thomas Malthus). The best of the academies taught according to the model established by the pioneering Philip Doddridge (1702–51): teaching in English rather than Latin and favouring critical reading and debate over doctrinaire instruction. Godwin's father had studied under Doddridge. The scientist Joseph Priestley – who taught at Warrington from 1761–67 – had been a student at Doddridge's Daventry Academy in the years immediately after the teacher's death. With a bursary from the institution's sponsors, Godwin joined London's Hoxton Academy in September 1773.

Godwin spent five years at Hoxton under the direction of the Reverends Abraham Rees and Andrew Kippis. Both were literary men, Rees an encyclopaedist and Kippis a biographer. As teachers, they were happy to debate with their students – Kippis too had been a student of Doddridge – and the two men's differing theological views suggest that the academy embraced a variety of religious positions. We see in Godwin's writing his commitment to open discussion as the best means of discovering truth, an idea that must have been born at Hoxton. It was his education at Hoxton, Godwin wrote, that had inculcated the mode of fearless intellectual enquiry that made him both famous and infamous in later years: 'from that time forward, I was indefatigable in my search for truth – I was perpetually prompting myself with the principle, *Sequar veritatem* ...' – he would follow truth, wherever it led.[6]

Godwin regarded himself as an outsider at the academy, his beliefs at odds with those of the majority, but he nonetheless made lifelong friends there. Kippis would later help Godwin find his feet as a professional writer, but it was fellow student James Marshall who would become Godwin's colleague, confidant and even occasional scribe, until Marshall's death in 1832.

Godwin finished Hoxton in 1778, aged twenty-two. With a good reference from the academy, he quickly found himself in what seems to have been a temporary appointment as minister to a congregation in Ware, Hertfordshire. It was here that Godwin made another friend – Joseph Fawcett – who the philosopher would one day describe as one of his four 'principal oral instructors'.[7] Fawcett was a younger man, but similarly educated and destined for the Dissenting ministry. Likely influenced by the great American theologian Jonathan Edwards, who considered only universal love – by extension, the love of God – to be a virtue, Fawcett dismissed the importance of personal affection. Godwin found the idea compelling, 'well adapted to the austerity and perfection which Calvinism recommends'.[8] The sentiment was reinforced when he read Edwards himself, but the idea remained with Godwin long after he appeared to have left Calvinism behind.

Godwin left Ware for a period in London, before an appointment as minister in Stowmarket, Suffolk at the beginning of 1780. For the first year, he had few friends. In 1781 Godwin made the acquaintance of a new arrival, a well-read textiles manufacturer called Frederic Norman, with whom he was able to discuss contemporary French philosophy. The two became fast friends and Godwin recounts that it was in this period that he read d'Holbach's *Système de la Nature* (1770) and experienced a series of revolutions in his religious opinions. The book denies the existence of free will and argues that belief in a higher power is merely the product of fear and ignorance. This determinism, usually referred to in the period as 'the law of necessity', was a profound influence on Godwin. Edwards too had denied free will, albeit within the framework of a divine plan – here Godwin must have begun to formulate his ideas of cause and effect, eventually arriving at the idea that thoughts and actions were usually the product of their intellectual context (thus, caused by society) rather than the result of individual choices. These theories would go on to have substantial influence on the philosophy that underpinned *Political Justice*.

Godwin laboured on in Stowmarket for just over two years. The circumstances of his departure suggest many things that would become clear in his published works: since taking up the appointment, Godwin had been in dispute with neighbouring ministers as to whether his right to administer the sacraments derived from the congregation, or from more established ministers. His flock had invited him to give communion and, after discussing the matter with members of the group,

Godwin agreed to do so without asking for the approval of the other Dissenting ministers of the county. His colleagues were scandalised by what they saw as the young Godwin's arrogance – there may have been some truth in this characterisation, as the philosopher's later account of the matter gives the impression that he thought it easier to obtain forgiveness than permission – but the principal at stake was a meaningful one. The community had chosen their minister, and that was all that mattered. The most senior minister in the area, the Reverend Thomas Harmer, wrote to Godwin to explain that unless he acknowledged their authority, his own would not be recognised outside the Stowmarket congregation. It seems unlikely that this troubled Godwin. He returned to London in April 1782.

With help from Marshall, Godwin made his first foray into writing. He planned his own periodical, a biographical series of great Englishmen, but the first instalment quickly mushroomed into a book-length project. The finished work, *The History of the Life of William Pitt, Earl of Chatham*, was published anonymously in January 1783. The work went out anonymously – not unusual in the period – but to later readers the marks of Godwin's authorship are obvious. The introduction makes impassioned claims about impartiality and truth and of truth's inexorable progress, all sentiments that would colour his early work. The publisher distributed the book to a number of major political figures, but it seems to have made little impression. Though he continued to publish throughout 1783, Godwin made another attempt at ministry, preaching at Beaconsfield (in Buckinghamshire) for the first half of the year.

None of Godwin's works that year had significant impact, but all of them contained signs of the ideas that were developing in his mind. A pamphlet defending the perennial parliamentary rebel, Charles James Fox, marked Godwin's lifelong admiration for the worldly, profligate politician who would one day prove instrumental in the abolition of the slave trade. A collection of Godwin's Beaconsfield sermons was remarkable for suggesting that faith should be subordinated to reason. Attempting to set himself up as a teacher, he convinced the publisher Thomas Cadell to print his substantial (fifty-four-page) prospectus outlining his approach to education. He failed to attract enough pupils to make a start in the venture, but Godwin writes eloquently about the power of literature as a moral teacher. Most interesting of all is a work called *The Herald of Literature*. Seemingly intended to show off Godwin's skills as a literary reviewer, the *Herald* comprises of ten reviews – each one an imaginary work by a well-known author. In each case, Godwin provides lengthy 'quotations', making a fair imitation of the more established author's style while offering his own praise or censure as reviewer (which, perhaps in a spirit of fairness, is based on general trends in that author's other works). The entire project is audacious and speaks of Godwin's dry (but sometimes absurd) sense of humour.[9]

The *Herald* apparently led to more work in 1784. The publisher John Murray gave Godwin work as a critic on his periodical (the *English Review*) and commissioned him to translate the Jacobite Lord Lovat's memoirs from their original French. Godwin dashed off three novels the same year, the shortest in only ten days. *Damon and Delia*, *Italian Letters* and *Imogen* are in many ways typical romances of the period – stories of rapacious aristocrats and virtuous damsels in peril. The philosopher likely wrote what he thought would be quickly accepted by publishers, as he and Marshall were often in desperate financial straits at the time. *Imogen*, however, stands out as another example of Godwin's playfulness: like *The Herald of Literature*, the novel is another 'hoax', discussing in its preface whether the work is a translation of an ancient Welsh manuscript or a seventeenth century fabrication. Nobody is likely to have been fooled by this; the 'found manuscript' was a well-known device in historical novels of the time. Viewed through this lens, the preface appears as a deliberately arch performance. Godwin draws attention to the story's use of Milton (Godwin rarely missed an opportunity to write about Milton) and makes extravagant comparisons between the beauty of the 'translation' and the best of Virgil, Homer and (another literary fake) Ossian. The preface gives us a taste of the vanity that was the philosopher's lifelong weakness, but it equally displays a playfulness and self-awareness that many of Godwin's later critics missed.

Kippis suggested to the publisher George Robinson that he employ Godwin as his assistant in compiling the *New Annual Register*. The *Register* was a Whig and Dissenter-aligned 'journal of record'. For an annual fee, Godwin became a political journalist. He researched his topics diligently, listening to parliamentary debates from the gallery and reporting with scrupulous fairness. His network of contacts grew. Godwin compiled lists of people he met and people he wanted to meet. Judging by the names presented and those underlined for emphasis, the philosopher sought the acquaintance of writers, thinkers and legislators that he admired rather than those that could advance him – the list he composed between 1773 and 1794 implies that Godwin was keener to make the acquaintance of actress Sarah Siddons and playwright Elizabeth Inchbald than he was the great Edmund Burke. Through the *English Review*, Godwin made the acquaintance of Joseph Priestley in early 1785. The *Review* usually took a conservative line on religion and politics; called upon to review Priestley's *History of the Corruptions of Christianity*, Godwin attempted to criticise from a position of strict impartiality, but wrote to the author to express his regard for Priestley's theological argument. Priestley wrote back to say that he thought the original review more than generous, and the two remained in occasional contact until the scientist left for Philadelphia in 1794.

Godwin's work on the *Register* (and another timely nod from Kippis) blossomed into further work on a newly established Whig journal, the *Political Herald*, in mid-1785. Godwin wrote letters for the *Herald* under the pseudonym 'Mucius', after the legendary Roman patriot who thrust his hand into the fire to defy a king. The letters were an imitation of the controversial *Letters of Junius* that had attacked the Grafton government fifteen years earlier, the identity of the author still debated to this day. As Mucius, Godwin attacked the Tories ferociously and in anonymous articles criticised Britain's exploitation of India. The *Herald*'s editor, Gilbert Stuart, died in August 1786. Godwin wrote to one of the journal's patrons, the playwright (and Foxite MP) Richard Brinsley Sheridan, to request that he might succeed Stuart. Sheridan was receptive but the discussion dragged on into the next year. Godwin was offered the job but Sheridan proposed to pay the salary directly from party funds. Perhaps concerned about the issue of editorial independence, Godwin turned him down.

The connection with Sheridan brought the would-be editor more contacts, but it was the publisher Robinson (who hosted parties for his book-trade friends) who around this time introduced Godwin to another man who would become a lifelong friend: the journalist, novelist and playwright, Thomas Holcroft. From meagre beginnings and with little formal education, Holcroft had toured Britain and Ireland as a travelling player, and later visited France as a correspondent. Holcroft was outspoken, forthright in his opinions and blunt to the point of rudeness. An exacting memory and an appetite for learning made him a vigorous conversationalist, delighting Godwin who valued sincerity and intellectual honesty above all things. The two sometimes called on each daily and could talk politics or religion into the small hours of the morning. Holcroft was a radical and an atheist, and his arguments led the already unorthodox Godwin to finally reject Christian faith in 1788 – the influence of others would eventually bring the philosopher back to the *idea* of God, but the former minister had turned his back on organised religion forever.

In these years, Godwin was a jobbing writer. He made a precarious living from his journalism and pestered Robinson for an advance so that he could write some 'great work' and make his name. He was occasionally a tutor and in the summer of 1788 he took on his second cousin, the twelve-year-old Thomas Cooper, as his resident pupil. The boy had recently lost his father, the family broken up and parcelled out to friends and relatives. Godwin, then living with Marshall, awkwardly stepped into a parental role. Godwin's relationship with Thomas was fractious – Godwin's tendency towards pedantry and a young boy's resentment at being foisted on a distant relative were an explosive combination. Yet the tutor admired his pupil's honesty, as surviving notes between them show (Cooper vented his anger at Godwin on paper and Godwin wrote back to commend him). The two remained together until Cooper was seventeen, when he left to become an actor in Edinburgh. He toured for some years and found success in the United States. Letters home to Godwin indicate a lasting respect and affection between them. Cooper would later describe Godwin as 'much more than a common father ... he has cherished and instructed me'.[10] Their relationship provides important insight into how Godwin's ideas on youth and learning developed over time. The philosopher's notes imply that he attempted to teach Cooper with the same strictness he had endured, only for his charge to rebel against it. In his reflections on his experiences with Cooper, we can see Godwin formulating the position that he would advance in *The Enquirer* (1797) – that an open and honest relationship between tutor and pupil was far more important than the specifics of what might be taught.

Godwin was a habitual note-taker and recorder of events. He appears to have written daily and his papers abound with pages of reflective commentary on his own life and character. It was in 1788 that he began keeping a regular diary (obviously a text of vast importance to his biographers), meticulously recording what he read, what he wrote, and who he met every day for the rest of his life.

Godwin's diary also marks major events, both in his life and in the world: 27 June 1789 records, prosaically, 'Revolution in France'. The revolution would change the course of history, but the reaction to it in Britain would shape the rest of Godwin's life. In the first impressions of Godwin and his associates, the revolution was a positive development. Radicals enthusiastically waved the tricolour and sent messages of support across the Channel. Many mainstream Whigs drew parallels between the French Revolution and Britain's 'Glorious' revolution of 1688 – despotic France was finally catching up with the modern world, they said, and would soon be on its way to parliamentary democracy and constitutional monarchy. Godwin and his friends were swept up on this great wave of enthusiasm; the philosopher later wrote that his 'heart beat high with great swelling sentiments of Liberty' and, remembering the great French thinkers he had imbibed since leaving Hoxton, 'could not refrain from conceiving sanguine hopes of a revolution of which such writings had been the precursors'.[11]

The Society for Commemorating the Glorious Revolution held an annual dinner on the fifth of November, the anniversary of William of Orange's landing in England. Godwin was a member, as were Kippis, Robinson and a raft of other notables that the philosopher knew or admired. The day before the anniversary in 1789, the society had heard a sermon by the mathematician, philosopher and Dissenting minister Richard Price that would become known as *A Discourse on the Love of Our Country*. Godwin did not hear the sermon, though he knew Price and attended the dinner the next day, but Price's address became instantly famous. Price claimed that 'country' was not a spot of ground but a community of friends, bound together by the same constitution of government and laws. To love one's country was not a belief in its superiority, but a desire to do good for those closest to us. To love one's country was to spread truth, virtue and liberty (the chief blessings of human nature, Price said). A country ignorant of these things deserved to be enlightened, a government that did not respect them deserved no loyalty. Price celebrated the principles of the Revolution Society that hosted him – religious freedom, the right of the people to choose and dismiss governments, and the right to resist the abuse of power. Though he carefully defended the king as a public servant who ruled by the people's consent, he attacked the obvious inequalities of British government:

> When the representation is partial, a kingdom possesses liberty only partially; and if extremely partial, it only gives a *semblance* of liberty; but if not only extremely partial, but corruptly chosen, and under corrupt influence after being chosen, it becomes a *nuisance*, and produces the worst of all forms of government – a government by corruption – a government carried on and supported by spreading venality and profligacy through a kingdom.[12]

Price described the American and French revolutions as equally glorious with Britain's own and imagined kingdoms across Europe 'starting from sleep, breaking their fetters' and the light of freedom kindling 'into a blaze that lays despotism in ashes'.[13]

The sermon rode a wave of popular enthusiasm, yet the establishment stood firm against the reforming movement in Britain. Attitudes began to harden. In March 1790, Fox led a parliamentary bill to repeal the Test Acts only to see it overwhelmingly voted down. When the French Assembly decreed an end to noble titles, the Revolution Society debated their abolition in Britain and voted in favour. In November, Burke published his *Reflections on the Revolution in France*, a book which quickly proved a rallying point for conservatives. In the past a supporter of American independence, the shock of the French revolution had pushed Burke into an increasingly reactionary position. He was uncertain whether France was ready for democracy and feared the consequences of reforming democracy too quickly in Britain. The *Reflections* are a defence of tradition and institution as a means of holding together the nation state. They are also conspicuously an attack on Price and the enthusiasm of British reformers. Radical writers leapt to defend Price and the revolution, among them Mary Wollstonecraft (then a member of Price's congregation). A war of conservative and radical pamphlets raged for months.

Still writing for the *New Annual Register*, Godwin devoted his main effort that year to a play – *St Dunstan*. Verse drama was not Godwin's strongest suit and the piece never made it to the stage, but its themes were clearly of the moment: *St Dunstan* depicts a politically powerful church playing on the fears of the mighty to cement its own position.

The first part of Thomas Paine's *Rights of Man* was published in March 1791. It was long thought that Godwin and Holcroft had a hand in steering the book to publication – close reading of Godwin's diary suggests otherwise, but the philosopher later included a cryptic reference to 'Paine's pamphlet' in a list of his early works. Like many contemporary works *Rights of Man* begins as a reply to Burke, but it quickly goes beyond that. Paine argues that human rights are not granted by law, but are instead natural and universal, going so far as to argue that the value of laws lies only in their power to protect the rights of the individual. The author leans heavily on the French Assembly's *Declaration of the Rights of Man and the Citizen* (1789), but makes no apology in applying its logic to the British situation. Paine denounces the monarchy as illegitimate, having usurped power by force of arms in 1066 and established itself on no better principle in the intervening years. The book outlines a programme of progressive taxation, wider employment, provision for the elderly, the sick and widowed, and free education for children. Godwin wrote (perhaps to Paine himself, or Holcroft – the passage has no address or date) that, 'the seeds of revolution it contains are so vigorous in their stamina, that nothing can overpower them'.[14] The first intended publisher (the usually redoubtable Joseph Johnson) had blanched at the possible backlash from releasing such a book into the world and the publication had been delayed until Paine's friends found a bookseller willing to put his name to it. Distributed widely, the book created a stir. The author refused substantial offers to buy the copyright, turning down a small fortune so that he could control the work's fate. Paine later insisted that the book's price be dropped to sixpence – well within the reach of any reader – to great consternation in government circles. For a time, Paine was the hero of radical London and the bête noire of conservatives everywhere. The reaction began in earnest during the summer. In July, 'Church and King' rioters in Birmingham sacked a hotel hosting a dinner celebrating Bastille Day as a prelude to four days of arson and violence directed at Dissenters and critics of the government – later dubbed 'the Priestley riots', as Joseph Priestley's home was among those destroyed. The authorities did little to quell the vandalism and the perpetrators were selective in their attacks, leading to allegations that the affair had been orchestrated by the government. Copycat violence occurred in Nottingham, Manchester, Newcastle and Exeter over the next year and a half.

The government's organised campaign against the radicals was still some months away and in the summer of 1791 it seemed as if Godwin's fortunes were changing for the better. He had proposed a great work on 'political principles' to the publisher George Robinson at the end of June and agreed a contract only a few days before the Birmingham riots. Robinson agreed to pay Godwin's expenses while the philosopher devoted himself entirely to condensing the 'best and most liberal in the science of politics' into a coherent system.[15] Godwin quit the *New Annual Register* at the beginning of September and his diary records months of dedicated reading, beginning with ethics and contemporary politics but later turning to histories, works on education and literature for insight. He wrote slowly but methodically, a few pages at a time. He began drafting that September, but would not finish for another sixteen months. The political debate raged around him, but Godwin's work would be one for the ages rather than a topical contribution. On 21 January 1793, France executed its king. The next day, Godwin put the finishing touches to his magnum opus. France declared war on Britain a little over a week later. Great political change was in the air. *An Enquiry Concerning Political Justice* was published on 14 February 1793.

3

The Philosopher
1793

Political Justice is both a timeless classic of political philosophy and a work clearly born in the revolutionary atmosphere of 1790s Europe. It asks important questions about the right to self-determination and how opinions or judgments are formed. It further questions fundamental assumptions about the nature of authority, ownership and the relations between individuals, in ways that remain challenging to this day. Yet the arguments of Godwin's book clearly emerge from a specifically eighteenth-century context and look out on the future with the clean-slate optimism that characterised the revolutionary period.

Political Justice is a difficult book to summarise. Not only is it a long, dense work that encompasses a wide range of topics, Godwin revised the book substantially only a few years after its initial publication and revised it again a few years after that. Any discussion of *Political Justice* must address the question of whether to privilege the philosopher's original argument or his final position – and later works complicate this further, some offering commentary on (or further revision to) the ideas articulated in Godwin's magnum opus. The book seems to acknowledge this, even in the preface to the first edition, arguing that 'the best elementary treatises after a certain time are reduced in their value by the operation of subsequent discoveries', and highlighting the development of the philosopher's opinions over the course of writing. That said, the core principles of *Political Justice* remain consistent through each of its three editions and Godwin's revisions are more concerned with adding qualification and depth to the argument than they are with changing anything fundamental in it. There is one notable exception to this: the philosopher's acceptance of a positive role for affection in stimulating and guiding moral action (in the later editions of *Political Justice*) that brought him many sneers from his critics.

The first edition of *Political Justice* was a sizeable text. Weighing in at around 800 pages over two large quarto volumes, the book sold at £1 16s – not an astronomical price, but one far outside the purchasing power of most people. This then was a book marketed as a serious philosophical treatise rather than a political tract (Adam Smith's *Wealth of Nations* retailed at a similar price). Godwin would later claim that he had avoided censorship (or worse) because the government did not believe that an expensive book could be dangerous.[1] If the state had indeed dismissed Godwin's book, they would in time regret it: *Political Justice* sold at least three thousand copies in its first edition and reached even greater numbers of readers. Many small political societies sprang up across Britain in the wake of the French Revolution, and a number of them clubbed together to buy copies of Godwin's book to read aloud at meetings and discuss. Radical publishers like Thomas Spence printed excerpts in their periodicals. At least one Dublin-based publisher produced a pirate edition. Godwin was quickly celebrated as the intellectual powerhouse of the radical movement. Looking back from the distance of 1825, William Hazlitt wrote:

> No work in our time gave such a blow to the philosophical mind of the country as the celebrated *Enquiry concerning Political Justice*. Tom Paine was considered for the time as a Tom Fool to him; Paley an old woman; Edmund Burke a flashy sophist. Truth, moral truth, it was supposed, had here taken up its abode, and these were the oracles of thought.[2]

The two volumes of *Political Justice* provide a division between the abstract and detailed sides of the philosopher's argument. The first volume sets out the theoretical position that Godwin had arrived at, outlining what the philosopher saw as a handful of irrefutable intellectual and moral principles about the nature of truth, happiness and human understanding. The second volume applies those principles to contemporary society and identifies the institutions and assumptions that hold people back from moral and intellectual improvement. Godwin's vision is optimistic and forward-looking: happiness is good and pain is evil – the most moral course of action is the one that brings happiness without causing suffering. Everybody wants to be happy; evil actions are simply mistakes, caused by incomplete information or insufficient consideration on the part of the individual. The philosopher's position seems naïve, but it allows him to frame moral error as something that can be corrected through greater critical reasoning – in short, that we can learn to be better people. In order to do this, Godwin argues, we need to recognise that our understanding of the world is shaped by the society we live in. Ignorance, inequality and privation may seem normal to us but, as sources of unhappiness, they are wrongs that can be put right if we critically evaluate (and correct) the things that cause them. We have not yet done so, the philosopher suggests, because too few people have been willing to look beyond the current system for answers.

The first volume of *Political Justice* uses a broad definition of both 'politics' and 'justice'. The philosopher implies that our actions are political insomuch as they impact on the community (most things do). Justice, Godwin says, encompasses all moral duty. 'Political justice' is then the operation of ethics within society, our moral responsibilities towards the people around us. Central to the book is the idea of truth as an ideal and an absolute. We should always strive to uncover the truth. We should never practise deception. We can find the correct answers to moral questions – perfect solutions that bring the greatest possible happiness while causing no pain – if we are aware of all the relevant variables and think about them hard enough (though Godwin accepts that this rarely happens in real life). In this sense the philosopher conflates truth with moral good. Things that we consider morally 'pure' (honesty, altruism) are truths to be discovered through deliberation and investigation. The philosopher writes about justice as a kind of deduction, the method by which we find the fairest and most benevolent course of action. It is important to note that, like many of his Enlightenment predecessors, Godwin rejects the notion of innate ideas. We are not born altruistic or selfish, but rather learn these behaviours from the people around us. If this is so, then we all have the potential to become happy, wise and benevolent people if we are willing to think for ourselves and act according to our own reasoned judgment rather than passively accepting consensus. Godwin goes further than this, insisting that we have a moral duty to act according to our own best judgment in all circumstances. The philosopher is clear about the importance of discussing our ideas and issues with other people, recognising that it can be difficult to uncover the right answers alone, but he is adamant that we have a responsibility to make decisions as individuals and not to take other people's opinions as our own. The search for truth is valuable in itself, we grow as individuals because we reason and act on moral questions, and we diminish ourselves when we obey without thinking.

Godwin considers the central principle of ethical decision-making to be the responsibility of the individual to reflect upon the issue at hand and determine whatever course of action will bring the most happiness and the least pain. Moreover, we have a duty to take whatever action will have the most positive long term effects (thus it is better to help a stranger in need than it is to indulge a friend who is not – a long-term relief from suffering is superior to a short-term gratification). This seems to imply a certain amount of moral arithmetic: a deliberation over the amount of discomfort we might be willing to endure for the greater good. Godwin sees this as regrettable and very difficult to avoid, yet the philosopher is not a relativist. *Political Justice* is clear that absolute, unqualified, good exists and that a thing cannot be considered truly good if it causes some amount of pain (that is, evil). This distinction may seem academic – as imperfect beings with imperfect knowledge, the best moral choice apparent to us may be far from ideal – but because the philosopher believes that such ideals exist, he is able to argue that we have a moral imperative to seek out the unequivocally good course of action in any situation and cannot claim to have done 'the right thing' unless we are certain that our choices have not led to evil in any degree. Godwin also considers the imperative to do the greatest possible good to be one that takes priority over all other concerns. Indeed, the philosopher argues that we have no other moral obligations: we owe no debts to those who have helped us in the past; we have only a duty to help those who need our help in the future. Equally, the philosopher claims that a promise should be considered no more than a statement of intent – if I give my word to do a thing but find another course of action will lead to greater happiness, it is my duty to do the latter. Godwin even goes so far as to suggest that the imperative to do the greatest good supersedes the bonds of love and friendship. True ethical reasoning (i.e. justice) is impartial and looks only to the overall amount of good generated by an action. The philosopher illustrates this in an example that came to be known as 'the famous fire cause' or 'the Fénelon dilemma'. In the example, Godwin argues that given the choice between saving the life of the great educational thinker François Fénelon or that of his chambermaid, we should save the former:

> We are not connected with one or two percipient beings, but with a society, a nation, and in some sense with the whole family of mankind. Of consequence that life ought to be preferred which will be most conducive to the general good. In saving the life of Fenelon, suppose at the moment when he was conceiving the project of his immortal Telemachus, I should be promoting the benefit of thousands, who have been cured by the perusal of it of some error, vice and consequent unhappiness. Nay, my benefit would extend farther than this, for every individual thus cured has become a better member of society, and has contributed in his turn to the happiness, the information and improvement of others.[3]

Godwin goes on to specifically dismiss self-preservation or personal ties in making such a decision – arguing that even if we ourselves were the chambermaid, or if the servant were a family member, we should still choose to protect the greater contribution to the general good. The philosopher's position was controversial, and many readers attacked its apparent severity, but Godwin here does no more than to point out the logical extent of his own argument. The philosopher himself raises the objection that we might reasonably prefer to save a person of known (good) moral character over a stranger whose achievements exist for us in the abstract. Godwin concedes that this is understandable but is, 'founded only in the present imperfection of human nature. It may serve as an apology for my error, but can never turn error into truth. It will always remain contrary to the strict and inflexible decisions of justice.'[4] The Fénelon dilemma earned Godwin the reputation of a clear-sighted but dispassionate philosopher, and Godwin's language here implies a kind of stern pragmatism that readers even today find alienating. Yet, although Godwin here makes a stark moral judgment, his conclusion implies that he saw the correct choice in the dilemma as an ideal and an absolute – we can accept that it is right to save the person who will make the greatest contribution to human happiness, but how might we accurately (and realistically) judge which person that is? Godwin accepts that, in the present state of human understanding, we probably can't. In the philosopher's thought-experiment we are omniscient (we know that

Fénelon is just imagining his greatest work); in real life, we must make snap judgments based on the evidence in front of us. The first edition of *Political Justice* is optimistic – it imagines that humanity might one day acquire the knowledge and wisdom required to make ideal moral choices, but its philosopher recognises that such a day is a long way off. We will never reach it without the gradual improvement of critical reason; something that Godwin says cannot happen unless we develop the habit of exercising our private judgment.

Godwin says that we have to make decisions for ourselves, but he urges us to discuss issues with other people before we take action. This is not a matter of forging a consensus – quite the opposite, since responsibility for the decision remains with the individual – rather that other people can help us (as an individual) to think critically. In discussion with other people we can test ideas, learn from someone else's experience, and benefit from an outsider's perspective, but the philosopher is clear that there is a right and a wrong way to go about this. Godwin holds that the best way to uncover the truth is through one-to-one conversation. The philosopher has many reservations about larger groups: they are often dominated by the loudest or boldest voices, not the wisest. Equally, public debate encourages sophistry – it is seen as a contest to be won rather than a means to uncover truth. Godwin sees private conversation as offering few rewards beyond intellectual satisfaction, thus both parties can be honest and open about their ideas, leading to a productive critical discussion.

Godwin puts honesty and openness under the general heading of 'sincerity'. Godwin argues that sincerity is our duty to always speak the truth and to openly volunteer what we know in order to help others. The philosopher's justification for this is practical: we will advance faster as a society if everyone shares what they know. Secrets hold us back – they essentially ration useful knowledge – but Godwin does not completely dismiss the idea of privacy. Though the philosopher believes we should live our lives in the open, he also argues that we are entitled to a sphere of discretion in our activities – I should not live my life in secret, but neither should others interfere with it.

This duty to act according to our private judgment leads Godwin to question the fundamental nature of authority. People who have proven themselves to be good and wise are entitled to our respect and consideration – we should listen to them, but we should not allow them to tell us what to do. Nor can they really make us. Unless another individual literally forces our hand, our actions are our own. To follow another's instructions is as much a conscious decision as any other, which means that the 'power' of even the most tyrannical authority rests on the acquiescence of the people it purports to rule. A tyrant might threaten dire consequences to those who refuse to comply with their orders, but the success or failure of this hinges on a mass of individual assessments regarding the costs and benefits of compliance. A more benign ruler might offer more palatable incentives for cooperation, but Godwin sees the process as the same: the individual makes a choice whether or not to acquiesce to authority, and always has (in principle) the freedom to choose differently.

If this is the case, then what exactly *is* authority? In a democracy, we might define authority as the power delegated to leaders by the consent of the led but Godwin is sceptical that any large group of people can really be of one mind. 'Leadership' is essentially problematic: for all a leader might be armed with the truth, swaying a crowd of strangers is more likely to hinge upon the group's confidence in the speaker than it is the rightness of his or her argument. In any body of people, each individual will have constructed their own understanding of the proposition in question. Some will have devised their own response, a subset of those may agree wholly with the leader but many will differ on points of detail. Others may not agree at all but find themselves unwilling to dispute an apparently popular resolution. A number may have no feelings about the topic at all, but will support the leader's decisions out of loyalty or respect (and this is not as small-minded as it may initially seem – we praise leaders who inspire trust and commend those who show loyalty to people who deserve it). All of this means that the apparent unanimity of any large group is probably an illusion. Such a statement seems uncontroversial if we assume the group's compliance to be an act of consent. Regardless of the individual's exact opinion, by going along with the consensus they demonstrate a tacit acceptance of another's judgment in place of their own. Godwin, however, considers a consensus of this kind to be precarious: if a leader derives their authority from the people under them, that authority evaporates if those people choose to withdraw their consent. Furthermore, Godwin says, if we have a duty to act according to our own reasoned judgment – and authority cannot actually prevent us from doing so – then a leader that claims to derive their authority from consent has no right to exert authority over those who withdraw their consent. The philosopher goes on to argue that we simply cannot, practically or ethically, delegate our moral reasoning to someone else. Not only is adopting another's opinions an evasion of our moral responsibilities, but Godwin considers it impossible for an individual to actually give up the ability to reason ethically – we continue to think, and to hold opinions, even if our behaviour is outwardly obedient. If this is so, Godwin argues, then one cannot derive power from consent. An individual might grant a leader or government the power to tell them what to do but, if that power can be withdrawn the first time the individual disagrees with their orders, said 'power' is little more than the right to make suggestions. The true power of government lies in its ability to use force.

> 'I have deeply reflected', suppose, 'upon the nature of virtue, and am convinced that a certain proceeding is incumbent on me. But the hangman, supported by an act of parliament, assures me I am mistaken.' If I yield my opinion to his *dictum*, my action becomes modified, and my character too.[5]

Governments exist because they have the capacity and willingness to use force against the individual in order to impose their will. Relatively benign governments may use this power sparingly but, though Godwin accepts that it is reasonable to use force to defend oneself and the community, the philosopher cannot condone the use or threat of violence to shape the behaviour of individuals. Few of us would sanction bullying, intimidation, or repression in support of political goals; but Godwin casts a net wide enough to question the validity of government-backed law and order. Governments have no power to dictate right and wrong. Authority, whether derived from a democratic consensus or the barrel of a gun, cannot make an immoral proposition into a moral one. 'Reason is the only legislator', says Godwin: moral truths are also intellectual truths, and governments are no more able to decree morality than they are to declare that a triangle has four sides.[6] What government *can* do is threaten (and deal out) consequences to those that stray from the path it has laid out. The philosopher is quick to point out that government has no moral right to do this. Since Godwin has dismissed the idea that government derives its authority from the peoples' consent, the philosopher implies that the use of force against transgressors can never be more than an assertion that might makes right. We might consider this uncharitable (certainly, few modern governments see themselves this way) and many would argue that non-tyrannical governments only offer force as a means to prevent or punish acts that are injurious to the community – it will always be necessary to maintain order. Even were we to accept this (and Godwin does not), it would not lend government any further legitimacy. The philosopher is clear that one cannot substitute authority for reason; 'because I say so' is an almost universally inadequate justification. Even in the case where government decrees something that is universally held to be true ('murder is wrong'), it lacks the moral standing by which to make that claim. The individual must still make a judgment on the matter for themselves. For Godwin, the interference of government actually makes the issue more problematic. Consider the hypothetical example of an accidental killing: I know there are no witnesses to the accident, so out of fear of being punished for murder, I commit deliberate crimes (disposing of the body, perjury) to efface my error. Later, I learn that the dead person was an outlaw with a bounty on their head, so I produce the body and take credit for the killing. Though the situation is unrealistic, it demonstrates how the threat of punishment (or the hope of reward) has the potential to distort the individual's ethical reasoning.

We can never entirely ignore the prospect of reward or punishment. Godwin's account of this is complex: while it would be highly virtuous to dismiss potential rewards and punishments as factors in the ethical process, a far-sighted cost/benefit analysis might conclude that it was reasonable to take steps to avoid punishment if said punishment would prevent the individual from doing good in the future (we should stand up for our principles, but martyrdom is not something to be considered lightly). In either case the individual has been forced to acknowledge the power of authority, even if only to discount it. Godwin argues that, by offering incentives to shape behaviour, authority pollutes our intentions and corrodes our ability to make moral judgments independently (based purely on the evidence in front of us). Over time, because authority's effects are ever-present, the individual becomes used to authority's influence on the decision-making process despite its lack of legitimacy. Individuals who are acculturated within such a system are likely to be brought up with an understanding of the ability of institutions or rulers to mete out consequences to a person's actions, but may never consider by what right they do so. The presence and influence of authority become normal, and with them (Godwin says) the habits of obedience.

Godwin argues forcefully that societies develop in response to the rules and expectations that governments place on them. A state that mandates military service will (over a few generations) create a martial tradition. A state that restricts the freedom of the press signals to the people that they should be cautious in their public statements. We might make the counter-argument that governments are equally shaped by the people – that laws and institutions grow out of society's needs and wants – but this assumes a more participatory government than the philosopher (who lived most of his life in a Britain where fewer than 5% of the population could vote) was willing to credit. For Godwin a government was as likely to be instituted through accident or force, as it was by popular will. The philosopher thus begins volume two of *Political Justice* with an analysis of what he sees as the main types of government, and the cultures they create around themselves.

Godwin divides governments into three categories: monarchies, aristocracies and democracies. Clearly we can see that many governments include aspects of more than one type, so we must infer that each category is meant to define the principal element of that polity. In each case, the philosopher identifies the contradictions inherent to each approach and the means by which each form of government works around its flaws to maintain the status quo.

Monarchy is, in theory, the rule of one individual with absolute power, but is in practice dependent on ministers to carry out the ruler's decrees. As observed in volume one, a lone individual lacks the capacity to enforce their will beyond the personal level. In volume two the philosopher extends this to the mechanics of leading a nation-state: how could even the wisest and most benevolent monarch understand the wants and needs of millions? Even with the best will in the world, a king or queen cannot investigate the problems of every subject in sufficient depth to be able to effectively help them. In practice, the monarch must rely on ministers to tell them the kingdom's problems and can only respond to them in what Godwin sees as arbitrary ways (we see in *Political Justice* an increasing scepticism about the value of 'macro' solutions compared with a detailed assessment of the specific case). The health of the nation is dependent not only on the virtues of the monarch, but on the probity of their subordinates. This, Godwin says, creates its own problems: in a system that invests final authority in a single person, the obvious route to success is to curry favour with that person. Such a system encourages ministers to attend to the monarch's needs ahead of those of the state and encourages the monarch to reward flatterers before more honest public servants. As ministers control the monarch's view of the world, it would require an unusually clear-sighted ruler to appoint advisors who could be relied upon to tell them the truth about the world rather than a mutually agreeable version of it. The system gives no incentive for ministers to do otherwise, and so the court 'bubble' becomes an intricate game of controlling access to the monarch while mediating the monarch's engagement with the kingdom. The philosopher sees this system as self-perpetuating: those ministers that rise to the top are those who are best at playing the game, and they in turn promote subordinates with the same qualities. The only way for monarchs to appoint honest ministers is to go outside the monarchical-ministerial system entirely (assuming that from their carefully managed perspective they know the option exists) but such outsiders must neutralise, accommodate, or negotiate an entrenched network of corruption and sycophancy in order to serve the public good.

Godwin discusses the monarch's insulation from society at some length, drawing on historical and topical examples to illustrate how the culture that surrounds monarchy renders anyone groomed for the throne into the worst possible candidate. Those who would seek to educate a future monarch work in the knowledge that their pupil will one day hold the power of life and death over them. Like royal ministers, royal tutors are better off giving in to their charges' wants rather than addressing their charges' needs. The spoilt pupil grows into a ruler who has never known failure, never known adversity, and never been told 'no'. They have no basis on which they can relate to their subjects and no experience of the world beyond the court. The philosopher argues, however, that the trappings of monarchy facilitate its survival. Keeping the monarchy separate from the people helps to disguise the machinery of government, presenting the illusion that the fate of the nation rests on the shoulders of one person. The ceremony and grandeur of the position lend a further impression of authority – titles claim that the instruments of state derive their power from the office of the monarch (realistically, the positions are the reverse), while pageantry is employed to 'dazzle our sense and mislead our judgment'.[7] We are encouraged to believe that one person can manage a nation, and Godwin argues that this basic falsehood underwrites all others. Deep down we know that monarchs are people like anyone else and, in indulging the conceit that one person can (and should) rule millions, we dignify every other form of dishonesty running through society. Further to this, Godwin claims that monarchy's culture of patronage and wealth trickles down to pollute every level of the community. If power is transferred through favour and authority demonstrated by ostentation, then everything (conspicuously) has its price. The philosopher grimly quotes Montesquieu's adage that 'we must not expect under a monarchy to find the people virtuous'.[8]

Godwin dismisses various approaches to reforming monarchical government: in what the philosopher calls 'limited' (implicitly, constitutional) monarchy, the ruler is even more wedded to their ministers because they have less power to replace them. Godwin argues that if a monarch is to be part of a constitutional settlement, they must be accountable or else a powerless figurehead (and the latter is dangerous because impotence encourages either rebellion or depravity). Elective monarchy, Godwin says, is known to be a source of political strife; the election of a president for life has many similarities. Godwin questions the need for a leader with executive powers at all. If a matter concerns the whole community, the whole community deserves a say on it. If an executive is necessary it should not have the ability to make arbitrary rulings. In any case, the philosopher seems to regard any attempt to mitigate the problems of monarchy as little more than an exercise in rebranding – monarchy is synonymous with corruption and tyranny.

Aristocratic government is described by Godwin as the appointment of a class of wise and benevolent leaders to act as moral shepherds to the rest of community. This class is exempted from everyday work in order to have the time to study moral questions on behalf of others, and membership is often passed down from generation to generation. Though he is even-handed in his explanation of aristocratic government as a model, Godwin is scathing about the idea of hereditary distinction: 'no principle can present a deeper insult upon reason and justice'.[9] The philosopher regards the idea of choosing leaders based on their ancestry as absurd, but observes that a hereditary leadership caste is even more problematic. If we allow the conceit that a leadership caste must have more free time to facilitate contemplation and deliberation (Godwin does not – arguing that a fair society would make that time available to all) then we must consider what effect this would have on those who grow up part of it. Godwin argues that a class that have led sheltered lives are ill-equipped to provide moral leadership because they have little opportunity to gain the life experience needed to be effective in that role – we might reasonably ask if those who had never known normal work would understand the moral dilemmas faced by those who experienced it every day. The philosopher goes further, suggesting that a long-term culture of ease encourages the accumulation of luxury and the associated ability to dispense patronage:

> Hence it appears, that to elect men to the rank of nobility is to elect them to a post of moral danger and a means of depravity; but that to constitute them hereditarily noble is to preclude them, bating a few extraordinary accidents, from all the causes that generate ability and virtue.[10]

Aristocracy is, in Godwin's view, both ineffective and unjust. Distinctions of class are arbitrary, and therefore wrong. The only honours we should bestow are those we award for an individual's own merits, chiefly their contribution to the moral health of their community. In an aristocratic system, the many support the few in return for leadership that the system itself undermines. Godwin argues that the dissolution of aristocracy is to everyone's benefit – those at the bottom are freed from injustice, while those at the top are freed from an enforced idleness (in some countries the nobility were barred from many professions) that works to the detriment of their character.

Godwin defines democracy as a system of government that requires only one regulating principle: the acknowledgment that all men are equal. In a democracy, every individual's voice should carry equal weight. Every individual shares the same moral duty to the people around them, and should hold the same stake in the fortunes of the community. The philosopher is quick to identify the problems that arise from this. While Godwin maintains that everyone has the same capacity for reason, he accepts that reason is a faculty that is developed through experience and reflection. If this is the case, then it is likely that the wiser members of any given community will be outnumbered by the unwise. A democratic society then is likely to be inconsistent in its decisions, easily swayed by the unscrupulous, and may struggle to recognise ideas of merit when they are proposed – all because the majority (who are unused to thinking critically about political questions) have the power to overrule an enlightened minority.

Yet Godwin argues that these problems are not inevitable and, even with these flaws, democracy would be preferable to both monarchy and aristocracy. Monarchy and aristocracy are forms of government predicated on the assumption that the people are not fit to govern themselves; before Godwin authoritarian thinkers from Hobbes to Burke had claimed that, without leaders, society would tear itself apart. Godwin, in contrast, counsels us not to assume that the character of the people in a democracy would be the same as under other regimes – other modes of government undermine the virtue and understanding of the populace (they legitimise dishonesty and repress dissent) while democracy enshrines the value of every voice and places individual reason above authority and tradition. The philosopher asserts that human beings, if allowed to develop the habits of critical reason, will almost certainly improve morally and intellectually. Godwin has reservations about elections and representation, so we must infer that what the philosopher describes here are the benefits of *direct* democracy (that is, where the people vote on every decision that affects the community) rather than a panegyric to any existing method of government. Indeed, while Godwin offers the possibility that representative democracy might actually provide the benefits claimed of aristocracy – the superintendence of the people by a group of wiser heads – any system that expects the individual to delegate the use of their judgment is at odds with some of the fundamental principles of Godwin's philosophy.

For Godwin, a true democracy is an equal society. A democratic government that grants more power to some than others is, the philosopher says, a democracy in name only. Elected representatives – if they are in fact necessary – should be regarded as no more than the deputies of those who elected them. Godwin tackles the idea of economic inequality in a later part of the book but notes in his discussion of democracy that an equal society is one where all have access to the same level of subsistence. For this reason, the philosopher asserts, a true democracy would never fight wars for gain – a nation where everyone has 'enough' has no need to deprive its neighbours of territory or resources. A democratic society may still need to protect itself from undemocratic neighbours and thus, in-keeping with Godwin's ideas on common moral duties, every citizen has a responsibility to stand in defence of the community. The philosopher rejects the need for a standing army. Separating the soldier and the citizen is to the detriment of society – it signals that to fight (and kill) is an acceptable profession, but one that we must keep at arm's length in a branch of the community with its own rules and expectations (i.e. military discipline). In delegating responsibility for its own security, the community invites soldiers to see themselves as the community's protectors. Godwin considers such a relationship unhealthy – there are obvious parallels with the principles of aristocracy, but the philosopher here is considerably more blunt:

> [the soldier] is cut off from the rest of the community, and has sentiments and a rule of judgment peculiar to himself. He considers his countrymen as indebted to him for their security; and, by an unavoidable transition of reasoning, believes that in a double sense they are at his mercy.[11]

The philosopher claims that a true nation-in-arms would be just as effective as a professional military. Mobilised citizens, who understand what they are fighting for and know that their cause is just, will out-fight enemies who lack the same confidence and motivation (and Godwin seems certain that only a democracy could really instil such qualities). The philosopher sees military training as a very simple matter, and claims that a democracy – since it will only ever need to fight defensively – could very quickly drill its army to the same standard as the invaders 'on the job'. Godwin dismisses generalship as quackery, asserting that a sufficiently educated and enquiring mind is all that is needed to excel as a military leader. Even if a lack of experienced generals were a disadvantage in war, Godwin says, it would be a small price to pay for the nation to be unencumbered with a military establishment in peacetime. If democracies are worse at fighting wars, the philosopher says, it is a point in their favour.

Godwin has deep reservations about the idea of offensive military operations, arguing that there can be no justification for a democracy to march outside its own borders except to render assistance to (Godwin does not say 'liberate') oppressed neighbours. Democracy's best weapon against injustice is the printing press; the philosopher imagines invading armies worn down and sprawling empires destabilised by courageous (and truthful) publishing. Coming at the end of a century where Britain had used military and naval aggression to carve out a global empire and curb the economic expansion of its rivals, the implications of the philosopher's argument were radical. Put simply, Godwin sees no justification for one community to interfere with the affairs of another, unless for humanitarian reasons.

Godwin is critical of permanent government institutions, up to and including parliaments or national assemblies. Though he accepts that communities will sometimes need a forum for public deliberation, regular meetings allow factions and cults of personality to develop – encouraging individuals to cast their votes according to their loyalty rather than their judgment. Godwin implies that it might be better if assemblies were only called when they have something crucial to debate, but it is the idea of a national assembly itself that leads the philosopher to question the intellectual and moral basis of democratic government itself.

Godwin regards voting as essentially problematic. Putting something to a vote usually signals the end of debate. The philosopher considers the purpose of discussion to be a collaborative search for truth – voting turns discussion into a competition that can be won, diminishing the importance of honesty and accuracy in favour of passion and rhetorical skill. Godwin – perhaps naively – believes that the truth will always eventually overcome persuasive flair, if the arguments are subjected to enough scrutiny. He suggests that debates should take place in multiple rounds, so as to allow time for reflection, and should continue until the truth is found. Votes commit the community to a decision based on the popularity of a measure rather than its fairness or necessity, thus encouraging sophistry and dishonesty. Godwin's ideal assembly seems to be little more than a talking shop, since the philosopher resists the most straightforward method by which the community might make decisions final. What gradually emerges from this is that Godwin is fundamentally uneasy with the principle of majority rule.

It seems as if it would be rare for matters put before a national assembly to be resolved with unanimous agreement, but for Godwin this does seem to be the only fair place for discussion to end. If a vote is considered as the resolution of a matter, and does not result in unanimous agreement, what is required of the minority party? In most democratic systems the 'losing' side of a vote is required to abide by the majority decision, at least until the matter can be brought before the house again. Godwin finds this unconscionable. Majority rule is not unity and voting does not determine truth. The philosopher cannot see any good reason why individuals who have voted against a measure should be obliged to carry it out. The dilemma is most easily framed as a matter of conscience: if an individual honestly believes a measure to be harmful or immoral then we would not be surprised to see them refuse to participate on ethical grounds. Godwin's insistence on the sanctity of individual judgment takes this one step further. If the intellectual and moral development of community requires that the individual always be allowed to exercise their private judgment, then the community must respect the objections of any individual on any issue. A government that expects the individual to conform against the dictates of their own judgment actually holds the community back, because a community that substitutes popular authority for the individual's critical reason teaches its citizens that their perception of truth is secondary to the will of the majority. The latter point seems uncontroversial in the context of genuine consensus. If (almost) everyone agrees that a measure is right, it may be that it has been explored sufficiently and found to be the best solution; the minority opinion may be inefficient or even harmful. Godwin, however, cannot imagine an erroneous minority opinion persisting for very long. Truth is, in the long term, irresistible – if a thing can be shown to be right, then it will eventually win unanimous agreement if the community is only patient (and, taking the long view, there will be occasions when the minority position is the correct one – time will allow it to eventually convince everyone else). A community that insists that the majority is always right inhibits the intellectual enquiries of its people by discouraging deviation from the norm:

> In numerous assemblies a thousand motives influence our judgments, independently of reason and evidence. Every man looks forward to the effects which the opinions he avows will produce on his success. Every man connects himself with some sect or party. The activity of his thought is shackled at every turn by the fear that his associates may disclaim him.[12]

A society that insists that its consensus is truth, and is willing to overrule individual judgment in support of that, creates a culture of intellectual timidity that resists moral and intellectual innovation. For a conservative government this is clearly desirable, but Godwin considers it an inevitable consequence of all political systems that prevent the individual from carrying out their duty to think and act independently. This puts the philosopher at odds with the rule of law, since even democratic legislation constitutes the imposition of consensus-based ethical guidelines intended to regulate behaviour. Godwin argues that if a law is not morally self-evident (outlawing a thing that is discernibly wrong) then breaking it is no crime. The influence of authority cannot make an action more or less wrong, so laws are at best descriptions of moral conduct (i.e. something we could have worked out on our own) and at worst arbitrary or immoral restrictions on individual freedom. The philosopher dryly observes that if laws were an effective means of making people more moral, they would have done it by now.

We might reasonably ask what the community should do if an individual's independent actions bring harm to those around them. We can infer from the way Godwin discusses wrongdoing that he imagines that it would be an unusual occurrence in communities that respected private judgment in the way that he outlines – the philosopher is sure that, if given the freedom to make every decision for themselves, people would mostly choose to live at peace with their neighbours. Godwin argues that if we take away external pressures on the individual that constrain their choices, what remains are some basic calculations about how to be happy. In Godwin's view, living peacefully and altruistically is self-evidently a better strategy than violence and theft. Setting aside the (quite reasonable) position that cooperation is a happier, more sustainable, way to live than predation; Godwin takes a different route. The self-interest hypothesis claims that all actions can be traced back to the individual's (perhaps unconscious) self-love. Godwin notes that this hypothesis justifies apparently altruistic acts through relatively complex or abstract logic (Bernard de Mandeville, the eighteenth century's best-known theorist of self-interest, claimed that bravery was merely a cover for one's shame at the idea of being thought a coward by observers). If such complicated reasons can be used to explain selfishness, Godwin says, then there is no reason why an individual left to their own devices should not reason themselves into benevolent acts instead. The ability to sympathise with others is, the philosopher argues, one of the most basic elements of human understanding. We know that, to be happy, we need the people around us to be happy too. If we help others to be happy, we will be happy ourselves and others will support our happiness in return. With sufficient reasoning, Godwin argues, the individual will always arrive at the conclusion that the altruistic course of action is the best one. According to this logic, wrongdoing – anything that causes a non-trivial amount of unhappiness – is the result of faulty reasoning, or reasoning based on inaccurate information.

People make mistakes, and Godwin argues that it is better to have a supportive environment to help people learn from them than it is for the community to take retribution. The philosopher sees a need for juries to investigate and admonish wrongdoers, but sees little point in punishing an individual in the present for an error they made in the past. Causing someone pain because they caused others pain will not undo what has happened, nor is it likely to prevent it from happening again. Godwin dismisses the idea of punishment as a deterrent – eighteenth-century Britain dealt out harsh punishments for even minor crimes, to little effect – and sees no role for it in reforming the individual. The philosopher accepts that the community will sometimes need to restrain people who are a danger to others (or themselves) but argues that imprisoning someone to prevent them from committing crimes in the future constitutes 'punishment upon suspicion' – the first step on the road towards tyranny.[13] Far better, Godwin says, to prevent crimes through community vigilance than to lock people up for things they haven't done.

Punishment and restraint are both forms of coercion, which the philosopher denounces in all its forms.

> Let us reflect for a moment upon the species of argument, if argument it is to be called, that coercion employs. It avers to its victim that he must necessarily be in the wrong, because I am more vigorous and more cunning than he. Will vigour and cunning be always on the side of truth? ... The thief that by main force surmounts the strength of his pursuers, or by stratagem and ingenuity escapes from their toils, so far as this argument is valid, proves the justice of his cause. Who can refrain from indignation when he sees justice thus miserably prostituted?[14]

As Godwin sees it, forcing people into conformity is counterproductive. Obedience is not belief; coercion has no power to convince someone of the truth of a proposition, only the power to punish them if they are seen to disagree. The philosopher's arguments against the utility of this have already been discussed. Fundamentally the philosopher believes that authority has no power to reform, only to corrupt. If something is true it can stand on its own merits; coercion can only alienate the mind from truth, in order to put something in its place. There are situations where coercion may be necessary to prevent a greater evil, but Godwin considers such circumstances to be few and far between: resisting violence, restraining someone in the midst of a crime, or defending the community from an invader who promises to bring injustice to the individual and their neighbours. Practicalities aside, the philosopher insists that coercion should only ever be a temporary expedient, and an individual responsibility. The alternative sets (for Godwin) a dangerous precedent. Were we to look on coercion as a duty of the community, it would impart a certain degree of legitimacy to the idea of using coercion against the individual in order to serve the community's goals – a position antithetical to the philosopher's belief in the importance of private judgment.

In any case, Godwin holds that an equal society would have little need for coercion. What is implicit throughout the second volume of *Political Justice* is that inequality in society persists because political authority is willing and able to use coercive force to defend it – central to this is the division of property. Laws of property assert and protect the individual's right to hold and distribute resources as they see fit, assuming they have laid claim to them without breaking the law themselves. We might expect Godwin to endorse this, since it seems to defend the exercise of private judgment, but the philosopher considers the accumulation of wealth to be morally wrong:

> If justice have any meaning, nothing can be more iniquitous, than for one man to possess superfluities, while there is a human being in existence that is not adequately supplied with these.
>
> Justice does not stop here. Every man is entitled, so far as the general stock will suffice, not only to the means of being, but of well being. It is unjust, if one man labour to the destruction of his health or his life, that another man may abound in luxuries. It is unjust, if one man be deprived of leisure to cultivate his rational powers, while another man contributes not a single effort to add to the common stock.[15]

We cannot ethically claim more resources than we can reasonably use, regardless of how hard we might have worked for them. Neither does our own success allow us to assert the right to distribute resources to others in any greater or lesser quantity than they need (we should support those who cannot support themselves, but we have no right to make ourselves into patrons). We could reasonably say that we have a duty to use our private judgment in distributing what resources we have acquired, but equally duty denies us the right to take more than we need or give more than is needed. A greater share of resources converts quickly into economic power – either through an unequal subdivision of resources (favouring allies over others), or through the hoarding of private luxuries. Godwin argues that the desire for these things stems from our need to be admired and respected by others – we seek an obvious symbol of our worth to display for strangers, or the gratitude of our clients for having favoured them over others. In a society that has no reason to covet wealth (i.e. one where no-one needs it to purchase basic comforts, or to participate in community decisions) then the individual can satisfy their desire for esteem through more virtuous pursuits. Without a constant need to acquire, individuals will only need to work as much as is needed to for subsistence. The burden of necessary jobs like food production will be significantly lessened thanks to an abundance of unengaged labour, as many specialist or mercantile professions are no longer required. The rest of one's time can be spent helping others, or improving oneself.

What Godwin advocates is the abolition of almost all forms of property. We have as much right to an object as we have need for it:

> What would denominate any thing my property? The fact, that it was necessary to my welfare. My right would be coeval with the existence of that necessity. The word property would probably remain; its signification only would be modified. The mistake does not so properly lie in the idea itself, as in the source from which it is traced. What I have, if it be necessary for my use, is truly mine; what I have, though the fruit of my own industry, if unnecessary, it is an usurpation for me to retain.[16]

Interestingly, the author extends this logic to our relationships with others. We cannot lay claim to another person, no matter how much we like them, and we should not allow ourselves to become attached to other people to any greater extent than they merit. The philosopher accepts that we are all social creatures, but argues that we should never allow ourselves to subsume our individual identity into concepts like family or community (or expect others to do so either). My blood relatives are not 'my' family, and I am not obliged to favour them over others because of any notion of shared identity. Godwin reserves particular ire for the institution of marriage, which he seems to consider the worst offender in this regard:

> marriage is an affair of property, and the worst of all properties. So long as two human beings are forbidden by positive institution to follow the dictates of their own mind, prejudice is alive and vigorous. So long as I seek to engross one woman to myself, and to prohibit my neighbour from proving his superior desert and reaping the fruits of it, I am guilty of the most odious of all monopolies.[17]

The philosopher's words held (for eighteenth-century readers) literal truth. The principle of coverture recognised husband and wife as a single legal entity, with the wife's rights suspended for the duration of the marriage. A married woman could not own her own property, or sign agreements in her own name; divorce required a private act of parliament. Godwin was certainly aware of this but, in-keeping with the overall tone of *Political Justice*, chooses to criticise marriage on a theoretical level.[18] The philosopher questions the ethical basis of monogamy: the only ethical grounds on which to establish a preference for one person over others is our perception of that person's greater merit – if that is the case, then what right do we have to deny the rest of the world the friendship of our favourite?

> The supposition that I must have a companion for life, is the result of a complication of vices. It is the dictate of cowardice, and not of fortitude. It flows from the desire of being loved and esteemed for something that is not desert.[19]

Godwin, perhaps still a Dissenting minister at heart, dismisses sex as 'a very trivial object' and denies any meaningful link between sex and 'the purest affection'.[20] In a society that has moved beyond monopolising relationships, people will continue to procreate (because it is necessary for the continuation for the species) but children will be raised and educated by those best-suited to doing so (rather than society assuming it to be the duty of biological parents). The philosopher finds it hard to believe that people would cohabit on a permanent basis, were we to do away with the laws and expectations that accompany the current system of property. Godwin argues that the tensions of living together will eventually make independent-minded people unhappy, implicitly criticising the everyday compromises that we make when living together (which may often clash with the philosopher's proposed duties to private judgment and impartiality).

Godwin regards all cooperation as a series of compromises. Working in concert with a neighbour requires us to organise our time to the convenience of both, and in doing so we curtail our own freedom of action. The philosopher calls this an evil, though for Godwin this simply means that it is a factor with only negative consequences (there is no upside to being forced to plan around someone else, though another person's aid may be good in itself). The philosopher's greatest concern regards the individual compromising their independence of mind: it is right for us to listen to others and absorb their ideas (through conversation, reading) but we should not submit to another's direction. Even if our collaborator can show that their argument is correct in every way, we must assimilate the proof ourselves and agree rather than simply conceding to our partner's greater wisdom. Tellingly, Godwin describes the practice of persuading someone to abandon negative behaviours as a form of punishment.

Godwin imagines a future where advances in technology and learning allow the individual to accomplish almost any practical task alone, but he accepts that cooperation remains necessary until that becomes the norm. Notably, Godwin does not see the community of the future as a primarily cooperative society – he dismisses the needs for resources to be held in common, since it is obvious to anyone possessed of sound judgment that they should simply give away their surplus to anyone in need (and fairly exchange goods or services for the same in kind). The philosopher seems to imagine that every individual will eventually become self-reliant. Godwin speculates that in the future everyone will be fed through only a small individual investment of time and effort, since the end of commerce and specialist employment will allow everyone to take part in food production (thus saving thousands of work-hours). Since the philosopher is critical of cooperation, however, we must infer that he foresees this production being an individual activity. This perhaps provides a glimpse of the future Godwin imagined: a society of peaceful, independent farmers that respect wisdom but not authority. It bears a passing resemblance to the Dissenting community of the philosopher's East Anglian childhood, albeit in an idealised form, but Godwin's vision does not look back to any kind of golden age – indeed, the philosopher is highly invested in the idea of progress, and speculates that a society committed to moral and intellectual improvement will one day conquer disease and old age (interestingly, Godwin sees ageing as a psychological problem as much as a physical one; greater happiness and wisdom will allow us to live longer). Humanity will spread out, the philosopher suggests, since much of the world remains uncultivated there will be room for everyone.[21] Greater longevity will obviously lead to an increase in population, but Godwin is grandly optimistic: perhaps without unhappiness, disease, or privation, humanity might live forever. Debate raged in the philosopher's lifetime as to what 'life' was – vital energy powering the body, consciousness, or the soul (to list only three common positions) – and Godwin thoughtfully quotes Benjamin Franklin's speculation that mind might one day become omnipotent over matter.

Without any need to procreate, population would settle at a manageable level. More importantly, existing boundaries on human improvement would evaporate. Death would never again deprive us of an individual's wisdom, nor would each successive generation need to be brought 'up to speed' before they could develop their own ideas. In short, the philosopher imagines a form of intelligence explosion similar to that prophesied by artificial intelligence evangelists centuries later.

The book's almost rapturous conclusion was in step with the radical culture of the time. In France, the abolition of religion in favour of reason was seriously discussed and attempts were made to de-Christianise public buildings and dispense with the religious trappings of state business. Across Europe, revolution was discussed in hushed tones as ordinary people waited to see how events would play out and monarchs raised armies to stamp out the French fire before it could spread. Godwin saw that British society needed drastic reform, though he remained a sceptic of revolutionary action. Most of his peers at the time were in favour of change, but few seriously advocated violence. Godwin maintained that the objective should be to change people's minds, not to force change upon them. He believed that it was necessary to show people the problems that existed outside their experience – he resolved to do this through fiction. He sat down to write his next novel only six weeks after seeing *Political Justice* to the press. He called it *Things as They Are*.

4

The Activist
1794-95

The government had begun to crack down on radical sentiments even before the declaration of war against France, issuing a royal proclamation against seditious writing in May 1792. Paine was tried in absentia on 11 December (he had fled to France months earlier). The prosecution claimed that, in disseminating the *Rights of Man* so widely, Paine had overstepped the boundaries of normal political debate – the implication being that to address the general public (most of whom could not vote) on political matters constituted an attempt to incite insurrection. Thomas Erskine, speaking for the defence, argued that regardless of whether or not one agreed with Paine, the exercise of free speech was essential to the political health of the nation. The jury found Paine guilty before they had even heard the prosecution's rebuttal. In the late summer of 1793, an Edinburgh court sentenced two men (the lawyer Thomas Muir and a minister, Thomas Palmer) to transportation for campaigning on behalf of universal suffrage. The convicts were taken by sea to London at the end of the year, where they were held on prison hulks until they could be shipped to Australia. Godwin visited them three times while they were at Woolwich, and wrote a letter complaining about their treatment (under the pseudonym 'Valerius') to the *Morning Chronicle*. In December, government spies in Edinburgh arranged the arrest of delegates to a convention on parliamentary reform, among them Godwin's friend Joseph Gerrald. They too were convicted and sentenced to transportation. In May 1794, the government arrested leading members of two reformist political groups (the Society for Constitutional Information and the London Corresponding Society) on charges of high treason. Among those charged was another of Godwin's friends, the writer and orator John Thelwall, as well as the veteran campaigner John Horne

Tooke. On 17 May, parliament voted to suspend Habeas Corpus, allowing the authorities to make further arrests without charge.

Things as They Are; or The Adventures of Caleb Williams was completed in the first week of the arrests. In the context of Paine's prosecution, the preface was confrontational:

> What is now presented to the public is no refined and abstract speculation; it is a study and delineation of things passing in the moral world. It is but of late that the inestimable importance of political principles has been adequately apprehended. It is now known to philosophers that the spirit and character of the government intrudes itself into every rank of society. But this is a truth highly worthy to be communicated to persons whom books of philosophy and science are never likely to reach. Accordingly it was proposed in the invention of the following work, to comprehend, as far as the progressive nature of a single story would allow, a general review of the modes of domestic and unrecorded despotism, by which man becomes the destroyer of man.[1]

The publisher (B. Crosby) panicked, perhaps when the scale of the treason arrests became clear, and the book was issued without a preface at the end of May. Many readers have inferred from Godwin's preface that the novel was intended to spread the ideas of *Political Justice* to the novel-reading public ('a truth highly worthy to be communicated'), but this reading fails to acknowledge the depth of *Caleb Williams* as a literary work. The novel is unequivocally a classic of Romantic-era literature. As well as being one of the first great psychological narratives – the story is told in the first person, and the mental states of both protagonist and antagonist are crucial to the story – the novel combines mystery, tragedy and political argument with outstanding unity. Aspects of the novel are obviously inspired by conclusions Godwin arrived at in writing his treatise: as the preface suggests, the work explores the application of authority in everyday life (by employers, within families) and its abuse; the novel's climax exemplifies the philosopher's conviction that truth is always ultimately triumphant. The relationship between the ideas of *Political Justice* and the ideas of *Caleb Williams* is, however, far more complicated than a literal reading of the preface might suggest.

The novel is a story of detection and pursuit. Caleb is a servant, working as a librarian and secretary for the aristocratic Falkland, who uncovers a dark secret from his employer's past. Though Caleb makes no attempt to expose him, Falkland frames Caleb for a crime to destroy his credibility. Caleb is imprisoned but makes a daring escape. Falkland employs a man to track Caleb down but, rather than attempt to recapture him, Caleb's pursuer is tasked with ensuring that his quarry is unable to flee the country but unable to settle anywhere within it – distributing 'papers' (implicitly a chapbook, the usual format of popular 'true crime' stories in the period) that depict him as a notorious housebreaker and master of deception. Falkland offers Caleb his freedom if he will sign a document exonerating his persecutor of his secret crime, but Caleb refuses to perjure himself. Caleb eventually forces a public confrontation and emerges victorious, yet is forever haunted by Falkland's destruction.

Many of the novel's episodes qualify or question arguments found in *Political Justice*. Falkland is widely held to be a wise and benevolent landowner (the protagonist continues to respect him even after suffering at his hands), and the case he makes in trying to persuade Caleb is that his life is ultimately more valuable than that of his servant – society makes a net gain if Caleb sacrifices his own honour to protect Falkland's. Godwin essentially complicates the Fénelon dilemma by bringing it into conflict with an equally important principle. Most notably, the optimism of *Political Justice* is undermined by the novel's sense that truth does not necessarily bring happiness. Caleb's victory is hollow because truth has destroyed a noble but misguided man. *Caleb Williams*'s greatest strength as a political novel is that it rarely lectures. There are moments of polemic when it attacks obvious injustice, but the text offers more questions than answers. Most challenging is the question of the novel's almost miraculous resolution. Godwin's original ending allowed tyranny to (believably) reassert itself, and left Caleb mad and dying in a prison cell. The published ending has stronger dramatic logic – it provides a satisfying conclusion to Falkland's character arc – but is altogether less realistic. The novel's original title, *Things as They Are*, encourages us to question the believability of its conclusion. Should it be read as a statement about the potential for change ('things as they could be'), or does it prompt us to consider why the ending appears unrealistic despite being morally sound? Godwin does not dictate an interpretation.

The novel was a resounding success, reviewers praised its power even when they could not bring themselves to approve of its message. The size of the initial print run is unknown, though as the work of a proven author, it was probably respectable. Whatever the size, it sold quickly, as Godwin was able to negotiate for a revised second edition (with a braver publisher, who restored the preface) a year later.[2] The philosopher's fame increased further. The government had not yet turned to arresting novelists, but Godwin began looking over his shoulder. He declined to visit Thelwall in prison for fear of being arrested as an associate, but sent him an (unsigned) letter of advice which the hot-tempered Thelwall did not take well. The full indictment of those arrested was published in October, with new names added to the list. Among them was Holcroft, who proudly presented himself to the Lord Chief Justice rather than waiting to be taken in. Godwin was in Warwickshire, the guest of one his many new well-wishers (the scholar and clergyman, Samuel Parr). As soon as the philosopher heard the news, he wrote to Holcroft's daughter instructing her to deliver his request to visit his friend in Newgate prison and to alert Erskine (who was again leading the defence) that he was the playwright's 'principal friend' (presumably for the purposes of consultation – Holcroft was, at the time, a widower). Holcroft himself replied in his usual argumentative manner, brushing off any need for Godwin's company and demanding that his friend focus on whatever he could do for the greater cause. The philosopher quickly went to work.

The law on treason was (literally) medieval, the statute unchanged since 1351. Since political authority of the time was vested in the body of the monarch, the charge of treason usually pertained to direct threats to the royal family. The government's indictment claimed that, because they wished to see the overthrow of the current regime, the defendants were guilty of 'imagining the king's death' – drawing a direct line from the desire to see a change in Britain's system of government, to the revolutionary overthrow of that system, to the killing of the monarch. Conservative and reactionary minds projected events in France onto the British political landscape, refusing to acknowledge the very different political context that had caused the downfall of the French monarchy. The government asserted that only parliament and the king had the authority to alter the nation's political arrangements, thus to organise an extra-parliamentary movement in support of reform was to act in contempt of parliament's authority. Since this, in the minds of the government, could only achieve its goals through revolution (and that revolution must inevitably end in the death of the monarch), then a popular movement for political reform must by extension be a plot to kill the king. The indictment accepted that peaceful protest was not a crime but asserted that the only legitimate outlet for this was to apply to parliament for redress. By extension, any political agitation that attempted to coerce parliament from outside (arguably this could include mass demonstration or strike action) was a form of insurrection.

Godwin completed his response inside three days and rushed it to the editor of the *Morning Chronicle*, where it was published on Monday 21 October, four days before the trial was due to begin. The publisher James Kearsley also arranged for separate publication as a pamphlet, and by the end of the day had been threatened with prosecution if he continued to sell it. The radical Daniel Isaac Eaton (who had already been prosecuted, and acquitted, for sedition that year) took over distribution and organised another printing.

The government's case rested on a broad, arguably elastic, definition of treason. Godwin's anonymous pamphlet, *Cursory Strictures on the Charge Delivered by Lord Chief Justice Eyre to the Grand Jury, October 2, 1794*, argued that the law was in fact quite specific in its definition. In typically fair-minded language, Godwin performs a scholarly demonstration of legal precedent – explaining how attempts to efforts by one monarch to widen the definition of treason were invariably swept away by their successors, thus creating no precedent for the wide-ranging interpretation of the law the government sought to use. The onus is on the government, Godwin argues, to show a direct relationship between reformist activity and treasonous conspiracy – the law does not allow one to encompass the other. Within a few days there was a conservative reply, allegedly written by the judge Sir Francis Buller (popularly believed to have been the origin of the term 'rule of thumb'). Eaton published that too, and Godwin's rebuttal. *Cursory Strictures* struck a huge blow for the defence. The first trial was that of London Corresponding Society Chair Thomas Hardy. The prosecution's opening statement lasted nine hours, an hour of which was given over to responding to Godwin's pamphlet. Erskine for the defence argued that the only people who had imagined the king's death were in government, that their suspicion had projected a malicious conspiracy onto men exercising their political rights. Hardy was acquitted after nine days in court. Horne Tooke and Thelwall were also tried, and acquitted, after which every other case was dismissed. The author of *Cursory Strictures* was a hero in radical circles, though only a few were aware of the author's identity. Horne Tooke did not learn of it until nearly a year later – Godwin records that the politician kissed his hand in gratitude. The philosopher was magnanimous in victory, and wrote (again, anonymously) to Lord Chief Justice Eyre to apologise for any intemperate language he had used in his pamphlets. It became clear that the case against the reformers had been built from reports submitted by a spy within their midst and the suspect, Charles Sinclair, was confronted on 24 November. The alleged spy was ejected from their circle, but Godwin took it upon himself a few weeks later to write to Sinclair with a list of specific accusations against him and offering him the chance to clear his name (though it is not clear if the letter was ever sent).

Godwin began the new year deeply engaged in revisions to *Political Justice*. The philosopher frequently tinkered with his own work, but his changes in the second edition of the text would be substantial. The first volume of the original had gone to the printer while Godwin was still working on the second. Despite the book's success, the philosopher was not happy with its argument. Godwin later wrote that a scholar did not truly understand a subject until they had written on it and, reading the first edition of *Political Justice*, we can see how the philosopher's ideas take shape over the course of drafting the work. The tone of the first volume is exploratory and questioning, the second clear and authoritative. The philosopher must have been conscious of this, because he seems to have returned to *Political Justice* within a few weeks of sending *Caleb Williams* to the publisher. Revision stalled during the Treason Trials in October 1794, but by the end of December Godwin was back on the job. Looking back at the work a few years later, the philosopher wrote:

> The *Enquiry Concerning Political Justice* I apprehend to be blemished by three errors: 1) Stoicism, or an inattention to the principle that pleasure and pain are the only bases upon which morality can rest; 2) Sandemanianism, or an inattention to the principle that feeling, and not judgement is the cause of human actions; 3) the unqualified condemnation of the private affections.
>
> It will be seen how strongly these errors are connected with the Calvinist system, which had been so deeply wrought in my mind in

early life, as to enable these errors long to survive the general system of religious opinions of which they formed a part.[3]

Godwin's clear-sightedness was not entirely the product of his own reflection, however. True to what he had argued in the book, Godwin's ideas were refined by conversation. He had, of course, discussed the themes of *Political Justice* with his peers while writing the first edition, but his newfound celebrity as the philosopher of the radical movement meant that his circle of friends had greatly expanded. Godwin had been professionally well-connected before, with many contacts in the world of publishing and on the forward-looking edge of the Whig political establishment. *Political Justice* brought him a wealth of personal connections, substantially broadening the number of people with whom Godwin could discuss political and philosophical matters. Godwin's diary records a host of new contacts: the Whig clergyman and teacher Samuel Parr; photography pioneer and pottery heir Thomas Wedgwood; financier John King; playwright Elizabeth Inchbald; essayist Mary Hays; and the poet William Wordsworth (he and Wordsworth did not get on). The philosopher, as detailed as ever, often notes the topics that were discussed. In the past, the majority of Godwin's friends had been radicals and Dissenters – people with the same perspective as the philosopher himself – and while Godwin did not forget his old friends (Holcroft and Marshall remained regular companions), the range of his new acquaintances meant that he was able to discuss his ideas with people who saw things differently.

Godwin discarded whole chapters from the original text and wrote new ones in their place. The bulk of the changes occur in the first volume, though Godwin made substantial amendments to the language of the later books and culled some of the most speculative ideas from the conclusion. The language of the second (and third) edition is more philosophical than that of the original – many minor revisions are clarifications or qualifications of statements made in the first edition, and the philosopher adds considerable nuance to his explanation of how the mind makes decisions. Most significant (which, as we see above, Godwin was conscious of) is his new account of the role of the emotions in motivating and channelling ethical actions.

In the first edition, Godwin had been certain that moral right was interchangeable with intellectual accuracy, that the best ethical response to any dilemma could be logically deduced and should be carried out because it is identifiably the correct answer to the question at hand. This, as the philosopher wrote above, was a remnant of his training as a San-demanian: the sect claimed that salvation derived from understanding the truth of the divine word. With hindsight, the philosopher recognised his own assumption – that we intrinsically want to do what is correct, rather than what pleases us (perhaps assuming that those sentiments were always interchangeable). This left Godwin with the need to explain motivation without undermining his concept of moral and intellectual truth. His answer to this problem is twofold: first, the second edition acknowledges that ascertaining the 'Godwinian truth' of a matter (i.e. the logically and morally correct response) is far more difficult than the philosopher had previously suggested; second, Godwin conceded that reasoning was not enough to motivate an action on its own – we have to care about the outcome.

In short, uncovering a perfect truth probably requires perfect perception. To deduce the ideal response to a moral dilemma, an individual would need to begin with an open mind, yet understand every variable of the situation, know the minds of the participants, and have enough time to reflect upon the possible consequences of their decision. In the second edition of *Political Justice* Godwin allows that time, experience and the limits of human cognition mean that few decisions are ever likely to meet this standard. The philosopher's qualification effectively places truth beyond the reach of mundane beings, rendering it an abstract idea that seems to have little bearing on the moral calculus of everyday life. Godwin's solution is to reframe truth as an ideal – a target for us to aim at, rather than a goal to be achieved. This constitutes a major change to the philosopher's position, but on an abstract level rather than a practical one. Godwin's principal interest remains the moral and intellectual improvement of humanity but, in the revisions to *Political Justice*, the philosopher now focuses on improvement as a process rather than an end. In every edition Godwin argues that individuals using their own judgment become wiser and more virtuous through the exercise of reason. In the first edition, however, the exercise of reason leads directly to truth – implying a kind of end-state where, without restric-tions on their reason, the populace becomes sufficiently wise to always act in ways that maximise happiness and eventually eliminate pain. The second edition recognises this as unlikely, if not impossible. This should not concern us, Godwin says, because the search for truth is valuable in itself. The philosopher claims that humanity has a limitless capacity for improvement. It may be impossible for us to perfectly deduce perfect answers, but the use of reason leads to *better* answers with every application. Reason may not usher us into an ideal world, but it certainly has the potential to make a better one.

The second edition's discussion of motivation and the emotions has more practical impact on Godwinian ethics. The first edition presents moral actions as essentially logical calculations – they are correct, and can be proven to be so. The philosopher's revised understanding of truth (as seen above) renders this problematic; without an accurate picture of the situation, our logic will be faulty. Godwin's revised account of improvement means that this is not intrinsically a disaster – we do the best we can with the information we have, and fail better next time – but it fails to explain why we choose to act morally in the first place. The first edition was able to argue that, the individual having deduced the truth, only perversity would explain why they would not choose to take the identifiably best course of action. The second edition, having undermined the certainty of this equation, instead argues that what motivates decisions are the feelings we have towards the outcome.

All actions ultimately derive from the desire to be happy – at the most basic level, to experience pleasure and avoid pain. Sympathy for the people around us means that these desires are not purely atavistic (we enjoy the happiness of others and share their pain). Reason organises and directs our desires; even an entirely selfish person must learn to prioritise needs over wants, and plan how to get them. Rather than concede ground to the self-interest hypothesis, however, Godwin argues that we very quickly develop a desire to do benevolent things (making other people happy makes us happy) and find that reason confirms them to be a productive and sensible use of our efforts – more so than selfish acts because, if we reason that other people have the same emotional needs as ourselves, we must recognise that an act that makes two people happy is better than something that pleases only one. In time we come to value benevolence itself rather than just its effects, becoming genuinely altruistic and not just a good team player.[4] In the second edition Godwin expands upon an idea that was hinted at in the first, developing a hierarchy of pleasures that places basic sensual desires at the bottom and benevolence at the top, arguing that more complex pleasures (e.g. reading) were superior to purely physical experiences because they could stimulate the mind and the emotions. Benevolent acts are not only personally satisfying but also propagate greater happiness around us, thus increasing our own pleasure further.

The revisions to *Political Justice* provide a straightforward explanation of why we choose to do altruistic things, and certainly a more robust one than the first edition. The philosopher realised, however, that the revised account of motivation was at odds with the earlier edition's 'unqualified condemnation of the private affections'. The first edition has a sort of austere clarity – our respect and esteem for others is secondary to the demands of truth and justice. In his discussion of the Fénelon dilemma, Godwin treats affection as a distraction from our real moral duties. Justice requires us to do whatever will bring the greatest happiness, and to consider impartially the question of how happiness might be increased. The philosopher argues that personal affection encourages us to overvalue the moral worth of the people closest to us, either because their benevolence impacts on us personally, or because we are more familiar with their contribution than we are with that of others. The second edition did not alter Godwin's commitment to impartiality – it is still better to save Fénelon over the chambermaid (now altered to valet) – but the philosopher acknowledged that the uncertainty of knowledge made such clear moral choices unrealistic. While some degree of uncertainty is inescapable, the revised *Political Justice* implies that we should aim to make informed moral choices over abstract ones. In absolute terms we should always help the person of greatest moral worth, in the greatest need. In practical terms, we can only help the person of greatest known moral worth, in the greatest need that we are aware of. The revisions soften Godwin's language considerably here and, although the philosopher retains his insistence that it would an error (albeit forgivable) to help a friend over a more needy stranger, the second edition displays an acceptance that favouring those of known moral calibre is a pragmatic compromise that still significantly contributes to general happiness. This may seem only sensible, but some critics at the time chose to see it as the philosopher retreating from an unworkable ethical position. To some extent Godwin agreed (as the revisions and subsequent essays show) and was publicly candid about having reconsidered.

The second edition's compromise opens the door to a more obvious change, though the philosopher did not see the immediate significance of this (and even his later discussions suggest that he did not consider its impact revolutionary). Conservative critics had found the first edition's commitment to impartiality disconcerting, since it appeared to argue that traditional values like loyalty, familialism, and patriotism were actually distractions from proper moral reasoning. The first edition had argued for the abolition of marriage, and that it was right for parents to give up their children to other people if those people would be better carers. The book had little to say about love or friendship, preferring to code personal relationships in terms of mutual regard and the respect due to individuals of proven moral quality. The second (and third) edition did not alter this to any great extent but, following through on the logic of the revisions, Godwin was forced to concede that personal relationships were crucial to the spread of happiness.

The philosopher discusses this in a number of essays written (mostly) after the revisions to *Political Justice*: it is implicit in his writings on teachers and pupils in *The Enquirer* (1797), forms an observation in the preface to the novel *St Leon* (1799), and receives a detailed explanation in a pamphlet entitled *Thoughts Occasioned by the Perusal of Dr Parr's Spital Sermon* (1801, now often referred to as the *Reply to Parr*). What Godwin concludes is that, if our duty is to create as much happiness as we are able, and that we should try our hardest to make informed decisions about how to do so, then it follows that the most effective use of our time and effort is to foster happiness among the people we know best. We understand the needs of our friends, family and neighbours better than we do those of strangers; we have a better understanding of how deserving our friends are of our time – how likely they are to do good as a result of our help. This serves to justify a number of behaviours that many would take for granted – prioritising family over friends, and friends over strangers – and within Godwin's thought it demonstrates the philosopher's journey from the abstract to the practical.

The political atmosphere of 1795 was heated. Emboldened by the failure of the treason trials, membership of reformist and radical political societies surged – the best known, the London Corresponding Society (LCS), led by trial defendants Hardy, Thelwall and Tooke, claimed around 3,000. In June the LCS held a huge public meeting at St George's Fields in Southwark calling for 'liberty and bread'. Estimates as to the size of the meeting vary dramatically: the LCS claimed as many as 300,000 attendees (a third of the population of London) while more sober assessments placed the figure as low as 40,000.[5] The government had assembled the militia over on Clapham Common, in any case. The society's address insisted on its loyalty to the king, and called upon him to dismiss the unscrupulous ministers leading the nation to ruin. The speech was less a petition than a warning. Another mass meeting in October used stronger language, accusing the king's ministers of high treason against the nation, and reminding the king himself that he ruled by the people's consent (because the Hanoverians had been invited to Britain over the Stuarts). Three days later, during the state opening of parliament on the 29th, demonstrators turned violent and the king's coach was pelted with stones – the damage was severe enough that the monarch believed he had been shot at and was forced to change to a private carriage. The now empty state coach was torn apart by the protestors.

Pitt's government leapt on these events as evidence that the nation was in peril, that new laws were needed to protect the person of the king and prevent violent insurrection. The *True Briton*, a reactionary newspaper founded with government funds, reported that the attack had been led by French agents.[6] The Archbishop of Canterbury authored a prayer for England's congregations (at the government's behest) that presented the violence as an assassination attempt. There were very few actual arrests, which radicals took as a sign that the government had orchestrated the affair themselves. Regardless, Pitt took the opportunity to push through a repressive legislative programme banning 'seditious meetings' and redefining treason in order to facilitate prosecutions. Pitt's laws are known to history as 'the Gagging Acts'. Holding a political lecture was to become a fineable offence, unless approved by two magistrates. Other political meetings required magistrates to be notified, and could be broken up if they were held to be encouraging contempt for the government. Refusal to disperse was punishable by death. The new law on treason made explicit the interpretation used by the prosecution in the trials of the previous year: that it was treasonous to express the intention to depose the monarch, or to attempt to intimidate parliament.

The two acts prompted a wave of petitions and further mass meetings, in London and across the country. Pamphlets, letters and essays flew back and forth. Godwin's contribution was critical of the legislation but maintained the reservations that he had outlined against revolutionary agitation in *Political Justice*. Godwin's *Considerations on Lord Grenville's and Mr Pitt's Bills* depicts the two acts as an attack on both free speech and free thought. The previous year's trials (and use of informants) suggested that the government could use the new law to prosecute any private discussion that did not endorse the existing political order, in Godwin's view essentially criminalising intellectual enquiry. In his donnish, qualified, way the philosopher calls Pitt and Grenville 'enemies of science' who threaten to plunge the country into a new dark age.[7] Yet the philosopher is critical of both sides: while he describes the radical movement's complaints as justified he argues that, even with the best of intentions, a passionate mass movement is likely to spin violently out of control. It won him few friends. John Thelwall took the pamphlet as a personal attack (one of Godwin's anonymous examples clearly refers to Thelwall, though the philosopher is not unkind) and the two exchanged angry letters. Samuel Parr wrote to express fulsome praise, but Godwin's reply is a reminder of his commitment to impartiality:

> I have offended some of my democratical friends by the freedom of its remarks, & could originally have no hope of its being acceptable to any party. But I could not, consistently with my feelings, protest against the tyranny of one party, without entering my caveat against the imprudence of the other.
>
> I should have been further gratified, if you had joined some censure to your liberal commendation. Authors stand in need of both.[8]

Popular protest was to little avail, however, and the two bills were passed in December. The LCS and other groups changed the way in which they held meetings in order to sidestep the law, but memberships dwindled rapidly. The radical movement continued, but without the energy or public support it had enjoyed prior to the Gagging Acts. The chair of the LCS committee fell to the gradualist Francis Place, who sought to place the society on firm financial ground. The small number of sympathetic MPs, led by Fox and Sheridan, continued their opposition through conventional parliamentary means (before walking out of the house in 1797) but distanced themselves from the popular societies. On 22 December, Godwin noted in his diary 'explanation w/Thelwal' and the two sparred (with less acrimony than in their private letters) in the pages of Thelwall's periodical, *The Tribune*. Their friendship was properly restored some months later.

The year 1796 would see Godwin make many new friends, but one of them would change the course of his life forever.

5

The Husband
1796–99

At the beginning of January, Mary Hays invited Godwin (with Holcroft in tow) to take tea with her and meet her friend, Mary Wollstonecraft. The philosopher was initially reluctant – he had met Wollstonecraft before and they had departed 'mutually displeased with each other' – but the engagement was a success.[1] Like many of Godwin's closest friends, Wollstonecraft was a radical author. She had been a governess, teacher, book critic and novelist, but Godwin knew her best from her political treatise *A Vindication of the Rights of Woman* (1792). He wrote later:

> When tried by the hoary and long-established laws of literary composition, it can scarcely maintain its claim to be placed in the first class of human productions. But when we consider the importance of its doctrines, and the eminence of genius it displays, it seems not very improbable that it will be read as long as the English language endures.[2]

The *Vindication* is framed as an intervention into the debate over public education in France prompted by the report of former bishop (later ambassador, and eventually prime minister) Charles Maurice de Talleyrand-Périgord. Talleyrand had recommended a comprehensive system of schools organised by a central authority but, while he had argued for the education of both sexes, he had advocated that women and girls be trained for a subordinate role. The French constitution of 1791 did not recognise women as citizens (and they would not receive full equality under the law until the late twentieth century). Wollstonecraft begins from the position that the supposed inferiority of women is a direct result of their infantilisation by education and culture. If women appear too ignorant and irrational to take part in the public sphere alongside men, it is because society has kept them ignorant and denied them the use of reason – the many negative behaviours attributed to women (timidity, deceitfulness, emotional fragility) are learned responses to a culture that shames, belittles, or ignores them when they attempt to participate in the world beyond the domestic sphere. Even were we to insist that the domestic sphere was the correct place for women to focus their attentions, denying wives and mothers education (or the agency to make their own decisions) can only have negative consequences for children and families.

Wollstonecraft picks apart the most influential texts of the period on the subject of women's education (she had published her own book on the education of girls some years earlier). Rousseau comes in for particular criticism – the Swiss philosopher argued that the ideal wife should subordinate her entire identity to that of her husband – but Wollstonecraft is able to show how even writers who are not hostile to women's learning, such as John Gregory in *A Father's Legacy to his Daughters* (1774), participate in the expectations of women's conduct that continue their oppression. Gregory understood an issue that Wollstonecraft is determined to explode: that patriarchal culture values what women appear to be, rather than what they are. Society expects a woman to appear beautiful, deferent and chaste – teaching women to value only the outward show of these attributes, because they are denied the education necessary to interrogate them for whatever virtue they might have. Wollstonecraft argues that virtue requires rational engagement; ignorance of immoral things merely provides a trap for the unwary while an educated understanding allows the conscious choice of good over bad. It is not possible for women to become genuinely moral beings while they are kept in perpetual childhood.

After the *Vindication*, Wollstonecraft had travelled to revolutionary Paris. Mixing with the English-speaking circle there she met Gilbert Imlay, an American adventurer and sometime novelist. They fell in love. They did not marry, but Wollstonecraft assumed Imlay's name and received a certificate from the US ambassador (as Imlay's 'wife') that freed her from the restrictions that had been placed on British subjects in France since the declaration of war in early 1793. In May 1794, the couple had a child, Fanny. Imlay's business dealings saw him travel extensively and, in April 1795, mother and daughter moved to London to await him.

Imlay followed later, but Wollstonecraft realised that his affections had cooled. Isolated and alone (she had only reluctantly returned to Britain) the writer attempted suicide, possibly through an overdose of laudanum. Upon her recovery, perhaps seeking a connection, she involved herself in Imlay's current venture – the American had helped to run a shipment of French silver through the British naval blockade, but the vessel had never arrived at its destination. The captain, Peder Ellefsen, had resurfaced but the silver had not been recovered. Mary travelled Scandinavia following sightings of the ship, and acted as Imlay's representative at Ellefsen's trial. To this day it remains unclear to what extent Imlay recouped his losses, but Wollstonecraft's journey was immortalised in her writing. Published as *Letters Written during a Short Residence in Sweden, Norway, and Denmark* in January 1796, the work describes the atmosphere of each country with a keen political eye while remaining alive to the great emotional resonance of the landscape. Godwin wrote that perhaps, 'a book of travels that so irresistibly seizes on the heart, never, in any other instance, found its way from the press'.[3] She returned to Britain in October to find that Imlay had taken up with another woman in her absence. She attempted suicide once more, soaking her clothes in the rain before throwing herself into the Thames. She was rescued by a boatman.

The meeting with Hays, Holcroft and Godwin came only a few weeks later. From Godwin's account she seems to have made no secret of her unhappiness. The philosopher wrote that from their first reacquaintance his 'sympathy in her anguish' was added to his respect for her as a writer. They met again at a dinner party a week later. He obtained a copy of her newly published *Letters* soon after that. 'If ever there was a book calculated to make a man in love with its author, this appears to me to be the book.'[4] The two made time to see each other: Wollstonecraft called on the philosopher unannounced on 14 April, in defiance of the social conventions of the time, and he visited her weekly for the rest of the spring. They grew increasingly affectionate. Godwin spent much of July visiting family and friends in East Anglia (where he reconciled with Thelwall) and wrote Wollstonecraft a wryly silly letter from Norwich:

Shall I write a love letter? May Lucifer fly away with me, if I do! No, when I make love, it shall be with the eloquent tones of my voice, with dying accents, with speaking glances (through the glass of my spectacles), with all the witching of that irresistible, universal passion. Curse on the mechanical, icy medium of pen & paper. When I make love, it shall be in a storm, as Jupiter made love to Semele, & turned her at once to a cinder. Do not these menaces terrify you?[5]

They became lovers in August. They met and talked, sent letters back and forth, as they struggled to express their feelings for one another. Godwin had clumsily courted women before, but genuine romance was a shock to him. Wollstonecraft was more experienced, but knew the knife's-edge balance of female propriety. Matters came to a head on the 17th, in a rapid exchange of letters. Wollstonecraft wrote that morning:

I feel that I cannot speak clearly on the subject to you, let me then briefly explain myself now I am alone. Yet, struggling as I have been a long time to attain peace of mind (or apathy) I am afraid to trace emotions to their source, which border on agony. [6]

Godwin wrote a confused reply:

For six & thirty hours I could think of nothing else. I longed inexpress-ibly to have you in my arms Why did not I come to you? I am a fool. I feared still that I might be deceiving myself as to your feelings, & that I was feeding my mind with groundless presumptions. … Upon con-sideration I find in you one fault, & but one. You have the feelings of nature, & you have the honesty to avow them. In all this you do well. I am sure you do. But do not let them tyrannise over you. Estimate every thing at its just value. It is best that we should be friends in every sense of the word; but in the mean time let us be friends.[7]

By the afternoon he had reconsidered and wrote again to beg for forgiveness. Before the letter could be delivered, the proactive Woll-stonecraft had called on him to put her feelings directly. Godwin's diary records almost daily meetings from that point on. The entry for 21 August reads 'chez moi, toute', a note that the philosopher's biographers have taken as a record of the first time the two made love. They kept their affair private, and saw their friends separately. Godwin helped to maintain the fiction of 'Mrs Imlay', addressing his letters to that name while simultaneously recording the correspondence in his diary under her real one. As writers, they read each other's work in draft – Godwin did not spare his lover from the bruising criticism he gave everyone else, but Wollstonecraft was more than willing to stand her ground where it mattered.

In the latter part of the year, Wollstonecraft was reviewing again for Joseph Johnson's *Analytical Review* and working on the novel that would become *The Wrongs of Woman* (1798). Godwin was completing a series of essays on education and literature, which was published as *The Enquirer* in February 1797. Though the philosopher presented the work as the conceptual opposite of *Political Justice* – an unsystematic collection of observations on various topics rather than a philosophical investigation – the book provides a significant insight into the direction of Godwin's thought. *The Enquirer*'s principal themes are reading and empathy, with a particular interest in how the two overlap. Education was not explored in detail in *Political Justice*, the philosopher was principally concerned about its power to indoctrinate and saw little scope for it as a method of moral and intellectual improvement. This initially seems counter-intuitive – we improve by learning – but Godwin's concerns stem from what he saw as (formal) education's greater utility as a conservative force than a progressive one. On their own terms, authoritarian, didactic models of education are highly effective – they impart an approved version of knowledge to a great number of learners, without having to engage with anything outside the terms they have set. Teaching someone to think critically is far more difficult. *The Enquirer* identifies the paradox the philosopher saw at the heart of formal education: how do we teach people to think for themselves?

Under the didactic model, teaching is relatively simple. The teacher imparts knowledge to pupils, and the skill of teaching lies in creating receptive learners. A more liberal version of this has the teacher training learners how to access knowledge on their own. This would seem to sidestep Godwin's concerns about authority – it is not dictatorial – but the teacher's understanding places boundaries on what the student can learn (I cannot guide you in learning things I know nothing about and, without guidance on how to evaluate a subject critically, a student doing research is merely swapping one fountain of knowledge for another). For Godwin, this is insufficient. The philosopher's vision of moral and intellectual improvement requires the individual to outgrow their prede-cessors, not merely to achieve the same standard. Godwin's ideal learner has the wisdom to respect the achievements of their ancestors, but the spirit to challenge accepted ideas when they appear lacking. The philosopher calls this genius – not some innate talent that separates great minds from the herd but a capacity that lies dormant in every individual, waiting to be awakened.

The Enquirer does not present a system of education. Godwin's essays offer few solutions but instead identify the philosophical issues that accompany different methods of teaching and learning. There are recurring themes: the relationship between teacher and student is inherently unbalanced; human beings are social creatures and need to share their ideas (in part, a need for esteem); our ideas and achievements should be regarded with humility and we should not be afraid to change our opinions when presented with better ones. Wollstonecraft's influence can be seen in the compromise Godwin offers for formal education. Rejecting both individual tutoring and boarding schools (the two most common methods in the period), the philosopher suggests that small day schools may avoid the worst problems of either method (Wollstonecraft had suggested the same in her own writing). Godwin regards schooling as a necessary evil, the least worst of all the systems tried: 'all education is despotism', he writes, acknowledging that teaching is something done to young people for their own good that inculcates habits of obedience rather than enquiry.[8] For all its faults, however, teaching encourages an intellectual rigour and diversity of learning that few auto-didacts ever develop. Schooling provides young people with a community of peers, which not only socialises them but also offers a social space away from the teacher's authority – space to develop the personal identity necessary to criticise or resist authority when needed.

Teaching remains an exercise of authority, which for Godwin renders it both morally and intellectually problematic. The philosopher suggests that reading affords the opportunity to educate without exerting authority over the learner. The text may dictate any number of things, but the reader is under no obligation to accept them. Indeed, all acts of reading are in some way acts of interpretation (at the most basic level, agreeing the meaning of words and sentences) and the reader can learn from a text even if they reject its message. For this reason, the philosopher dismisses the idea that books can ever genuinely corrupt someone – a work may celebrate odious things, but it has no power to make the reader emulate them. The author considers all literature to be instructive because it enables the reader to exercise their imagination, putting themselves in the place of the literary protagonist (fictional, historical or authorial) to experience something akin to a simulation of the character's experience. We feel what they feel, and learn from it.

In December 1796, Wollstonecraft began to suspect that she was pregnant with Godwin's child. The couple quarrelled. The notes that passed between them afterwards show Godwin hurt by her apparent regrets, but they patched things up quickly. Wollstonecraft was likely under pressure to settle debts she had accrued during her separation from Imlay, and the prospect of becoming an unmarried mother for the second time cannot have aided her peace of mind. In the spring, Godwin borrowed money from Thomas Wedgwood to pay Wollstonecraft's creditors and the couple resolved to marry. The wedding was held at St Pancras on 29 March, with Marshall as the only witness. They moved in together at the Polygon in Somers Town (then on the north edge of London) on 6 April, but Godwin rented rooms a few streets away in order to have his own space to work. They informed their friends slowly and with apparent reluctance. Holcroft wished them the utmost happiness but was clearly saddened at having been left out of the secret. An embarrassed letter from Godwin to Wedgwood requested more money on Wollstonecraft's behalf and attempted to justify his marriage in the light of his vehement criticism of the institution itself:

> Nothing but a regard for the happiness of the individual, which I had no right to injure, could have induced me to submit to an institution, which I wish to see abolished, & which I would recommend to my fellow men, never to practise, but with the greatest caution. Having done what I thought necessary for the peace & respectability of the individual, I hold myself no otherwise bound than I was before the ceremony took place.[9]

Godwin's anxiety regarding Wollstonecraft's 'respectability' was well-founded. Though the marriage may have shielded her from some of the opprobrium reserved for unmarried mothers, the pretence of her marriage to Imlay was entirely exploded. According to Godwin, this was not any great revelation: Wollstonecraft was candid in explaining her relationship with Imlay, even to casual acquaintances, and did not seem to fear it being widely known.[10] Godwin reports that Wollstonecraft and her friends persisted in using 'Mrs Imlay' out of convenience rather than deception. Indeed, Godwin's awkward attempt to irreverently inform Mary Hays of their marriage refers to the wedding as the obvious way for Wollstonecraft to drop the Imlay name, suggesting that they had discussed the practical concerns of doing so.[11] Some of their acquaintances took the opportunity to cut ties with the couple regardless, which Godwin took as an adherence to the form of proper behaviour rather than its spirit. Chief among those cutting ties was Elizabeth Inchbald. Formerly a close friend of Godwin, rumour implied that the playwright may have resented 'losing' the philosopher to another woman. Yet Inchbald was often guarded in her social and political engagements (an important survival trait for a woman in the highly public world of theatre) and may have thought the loss of Godwin's friendship an acceptable sacrifice to minimise her association with any potential scandal.

Godwin and Wollstonecraft both took care to maintain a degree of independence from one another. Godwin's rented rooms were more than just an office, and the philosopher sometimes slept there, the couple communicating through notes and letters in much the same way as they had before their marriage. They saw their friends separately (radical in a time when many considered it improper for wives to speak to men without their husbands present). Wollstonecraft wrote to their mutual friend Amelia Alderson, 'in short, I still mean to be independent, even to the cultivating sentiments and principles in my children's minds (should I have more), which he disavows'.[12] Yet some degree of domesticity crept in. The couple were happy and Godwin doted on Fanny, now his stepdaughter. The notes suggest that their relationship thrived on blunt honesty. Though Wollstonecraft expressed reservations about her husband's doctrine of sincerity, she was open about her feelings. Complaining of having missed an opportunity to walk in the country with friends because of a prior engagement with Godwin's sister, the couple apparently argued. Wollstonecraft later wrote to him:

> I am sorry we entered on an altercation this morning, which probably has led us both to justify ourselves at the expence of the other. Perfect confidence, and sincerity of action is, I am persuaded, incompatible with the present state of reason. I am sorry for the bitterness of your expressions when you denominated, what I think a just contempt of a false principle of action, *savage resentment, and the worst of vices,*

not because I winced under the lash, but as it led me to infer that the coquettish candour of vanity was a much less generous motive. I know that respect is the shadow of wealth, and commonly obtained, when that is wanted, by a criminal compliance with the prejudice of society.[13]

In June, Godwin took a trip to the Midlands to visit Wedgwood and see his potteries. His letters home speak volumes about the sort of warm and affectionate family the Godwins had so quickly become – most letters feature a passage for Fanny, including an ongoing discussion about the whereabouts of a misplaced toy. It is clear that Wollstonecraft missed him dearly; her last letter before his return complains that the tenderness of his letters had 'evaporated' the longer he had been away (he arrived home the next day).[14]

Wollstonecraft went into labour at 5 a.m. on Wednesday 30 August 1797. She was confident, casually writing notes to Godwin (who had been sent to his rooms until the birth was completed) until the pains encouraged her to retire to bed. She was attended by an experienced midwife (Mrs Blenkinsop of the Westminster Lying-In Hospital, a place for poorer women) but the labour continued for many hours. Mary Wollstonecraft gave birth to Mary Wollstonecraft Godwin at 11.20 p.m. Complications presented themselves a few hours later: the mother had not expelled the placenta. Still a concern today, in the eighteenth century it quickly led to infection and death. Godwin summoned Blenkinsop's surgeon colleague, Dr Poignand, who removed the placenta surgically in the small hours of the Thursday, causing significant blood loss. For Wollstonecraft the experience was agonising. Godwin sent for another doctor, his wife's friend George Fordyce, who pronounced 'no particular cause of alarm'.[15] For a few days, life seemed to return to normal. Godwin went about some pressing business on Friday, certain that his wife was recovering strongly. On Sunday, Wollstonecraft was overcome with fits of shivering so violent that she later described them as a struggle between life and death. Some of the placenta apparently remained and had become infected. Poignand and Fordyce were both summoned again; Poignand refused to attend because another physician had been consulted, but Fordyce (by Tuesday) had called in another doctor – John Clark, London's most senior midwifery practitioner – with a view to further surgery. The doctors presumably decided against another procedure, advising Godwin only to give his wife wine for the pain. By Wednesday 6 September it was clear that Wollstonecraft was not long for this world, but she throughout bore her suffering with patience and calm. Godwin, by contrast, was far from his usual rational self. He begged his friend Basil Montagu to find a new doctor. Montagu turned to Godwin's friend Anthony Carlisle. Carlisle was that day dining some miles outside London, but Montagu tracked him down and brought him to Wollstone-craft's side. Carlisle stayed with them until the end. Godwin's account lists all those who visited or helped in his wife's last days. She appeared to rally and held on until Sunday morning, twelve days after having given birth. On her last full day she discussed with Godwin what she wanted for her daughters, though what precisely was said we can only infer from her writing. Godwin's diary records her death simply with the words '20 minutes before 8', underlined twice. She was buried at St Pancras, the church where they were married. Godwin was too distraught to attend.

Godwin mourned Wollstonecraft as a fellow author. With the help of Joseph Johnson and the Robinsons, he published the unfinished *Wrongs of Woman* alongside some of her letters and fragments. At the same time, and within days of the funeral, he was back at his desk writing Woll-stonecraft's life story. He worked on it in bursts over the subsequent weeks, finishing it in mid-November and publishing it through Johnson in January 1798. The *Memoirs of the Author of a Vindication of the Rights of Woman* are deeply personal, and distinctively Godwin. The philosopher's love and admiration for Wollstonecraft can be seen on every page, but the text does not shy away from the bracing honesty that characterised their relationship. Godwin told of her father's cruelty and her mother's strictness; her fervent passion for her friend Fanny Blood; her love for the (married) painter, Henry Fuseli; her child out of wedlock with Imlay; and her two suicide attempts. Biography in the period was primarily a celebration of the subject's life – no doubt Godwin saw the work as such – but it was common to draw a veil over episodes that might be deemed controversial. From the *Memoir*'s foreword we might infer that the phi-losopher's intention was to lay to rest painful and misleading rumours about Wollstonecraft's life by providing the whole and unvarnished truth. Godwin hid nothing, nor did he flinch from describing her flaws as well as the genius that he saw in her character. For all the research that the philosopher attempted in writing Wollstonecraft's life (her sisters, among others, were not forthcoming in their help) his portrait of her is subjective. The *Memoir* paints Wollstonecraft as Godwin saw her, and in relation to how he saw himself: she is a passionate, intuitive, imaginative spirit contrasted with his rational, logical, sceptical intellect. He credits her with teaching him the value of imagination. Godwin at times seems to construct Wollstonecraft as a woman of sensibility – a mind, 'almost of too fine a texture to encounter the vicissitudes of human affairs, to whom pleasure is transport, and disappointment is agony indescribable'.[16] She might not have appreciated the description, having rejected sensibility (in its negative sense, valuing the display of emotion over reason) in the *Vindication* as a culture that enervated women. In the *Vindication* Wollstonecraft argued that sensibility celebrated the irrational – reinforcing existing stereotypes of women's abilities – instead of encouraging women to think for themselves. Yet in the *Letters from Sweden* the author offers a new kind of sensibility: the combination of emotional literacy and critical thought that would come to mark the literature of the new century.

Godwin regards Wollstonecraft's sensibility to have been the force behind her sound moral intuition. Godwin's sketch of his wife's character ties closely with the philosopher's revised understanding of ethical decision-making in *Political Justice*, both that we need to feel in order to motivate moral actions, and that empathy is fundamental to doing so. The philosopher began his revisions to *Political Justice* long before he became reacquainted with Wollstonecraft in 1796, but in the *Memoir* Godwin credits his wife with teaching him the meaning of feeling and imagination.

We might observe that Godwin's description of their contrasting but complementary personalities falls into traditional gender roles – he thinks, she feels – but the *Memoir* depicts their relationship as one of equal respect and partnership. What is clear from the text is how much the couple shared:

> Mary rested her head upon the shoulder of her lover, hoping to find a heart with which she might safely treasure her world of affection; fearing to commit a mistake, yet, in spite of her melancholy experience, fraught with that generous confidence, which, in a great soul, is never extinguished. I had never loved till now; or, at least, had never nourished a passion to the same growth, or met with an object so consummately worthy.[17]

While the philosopher draws attention to the steps both took to preserve their independence, consistent with Godwin's views on cohabitation, his description of their happiness strongly resembles Wollstonecraft's views on companionship. In the *Vindication* Wollstonecraft insists that men and women are different, but morally and intellectually equal. Godwin would come to adopt similar, but more problematic views.

The response to Godwin's biography was hostile, sometimes violently so. Conservative commentators revelled in what they considered the sordid details of Wollstonecraft's life, leaping on the details of her romantic affairs as evidence of her flagrant immorality. A reactionary satire in the pages of the *Anti-Jacobin* magazine insinuated that Godwin had covered up further 'crimes', and slandered her as a traitor and a prostitute. Less ideological critics affected shock at the candour of Godwin's writing. It was conventional to use biography as an apology for an unconventional life, emphasising deathbed piety and repentance. Nothing in the *Memoir* suggests that Godwin saw any need for forgiveness; the philosopher's pride in his wife's achievements is palpable, and his commentary on her mistakes is not judgmental. The *Memoir* does not seek pity, denying readers their traditional prerogative to absolve the subject's 'sins' as a precursor to acknowledging their contribution. A work that confounds expectations often alienates readers, and so it was for Godwin's biography. The *Memoir* forced readers to either admire or condemn its subject, and to admire Wollstonecraft was to reject society's expectations regarding sex, marriage and gender. Few had the courage. Some persons named in the biography threatened Godwin with legal action, and Johnson hurriedly issued a second edition with names excised. Godwin took the opportunity to rephrase or add a number of passages on happiness and companionship, taking him still further away from the austerity of the earliest *Political Justice*. Ironically, many readers took the *Memoir*'s honesty as evidence of Godwin's emotional distance – imagining that some cold-hearted dedication to truth had outweighed the 'natural' impulse to protect Wollstonecraft's memory. The abolitionist (and friend of Fuseli) William Roscoe wrote privately in her honour:

> Hard was thy fate in all the scenes of life,
> As daughter, sister, parent, friend and wife
> But harder still in death thy fate we own,
> Mourn'd by thy Godwin – with a heart of stone.[18]

Attacks on Godwin himself began to mount, and not simply as a result of the *Memoir*. He was caricatured in fiction: a slew of reactionary novels featured unfeeling philosophers as either villains or foils.[19] Gillray's cartoons placed him among a rogue's gallery of Jacobin grotesques (his 1798 tableau 'New Morality' has a braying ass reading from *Political Justice*; he appeared again in 1800's 'The Apples and the Horse-Turds'). Magazines and newspapers satirised him in verse. A handful of conservative thinkers attempted to engage with and combat Godwin's ideas. In June 1798 Johnson published a short (initially anonymous) work on population growth by a Surrey clergyman called Thomas Robert Malthus. *An Essay on the Principle of Population* argued that unchecked populations grew geometrically (doubling every generation) but food production could only grow arithmetically – a slow increase that was quickly outstripped by the number of mouths it needed to feed. Malthus theorised that famine and disease were natural checks that prevented significant overpopulation; the misery suffered by the poor in times of want was unavoidable, he claimed, because attempts to alleviate it only created the conditions for more serious crises in the future. Malthus argued that Poor Relief caused inflation, making everyone poorer, and that the multiplication of poor families inevitably led to mass starvation in times of bad harvest. Much of the latter part of the *Essay* was written in reply to *Political Justice* (and to a lesser extent, *The Enquirer*). Malthus's address to Godwin is collegial and flattering, calling the philosopher's system of equality, 'by far the most beautiful and engaging of any that has yet appeared'.[20] Yet Malthus airily rejects the majority of Godwin's thesis, arguing that poverty and misery are essentially natural phenomena rather than the product of social inequality. He considers Godwin's enlightened future to be dangerously naïve: the abolition of marriage would lead to rampant promiscuity and uncontrolled population growth; the equalisation of property would only demonstrate that there was insufficient usable land to support the population in equal levels of comfort. Central to Malthus's argument is the assumption that a fair and just society would fail catastrophically without the checks that present (unjust) society provides.

Godwin read the *Essay* with great interest and met its author at a dinner party held by Johnson a week later. Malthus and Godwin seem to have found much to discuss – they met again for breakfast the next day, and exchanged letters in the following week. The correspondence serves as a reminder as to how little empirical data existed on the subject at the

Figure 2   James Gillray's cartoon, 'New morality; – or – the promis'd installment of the high-priest of the Theophilanthropes, with the homage of Leviathan and his suite' (1798). The print depicts a host of radical celebrities of the period – the phrygian caps are a symbol of their supposed adherence to French revolutionary ideas.

(National Portrait Gallery, London)

time: Godwin believes the population to be falling, Malthus claims that it is increasing, but both base their assertions on (inaccurate) information gathered by Richard Price over a decade earlier. Both men would return to the debate many times over the subsequent years. Malthus revised and expanded the *Essay* five times over the next thirty years, each time adding more data to support his theory. The second edition (1803) shows signs of Godwin's influence, arguing that it might be possible to actively manage the birth rate through 'moral restraint' (recalling *Political Justice*'s speculation that people might simply choose not to procreate if they saw no need), and their interactions remained cordial for many years. Malthus was, however, fundamentally conservative. He wrote to Godwin that:

> I only approve of the present form of society, because I cannot myself, according to the laws of just theory, see any other form, that can, consistent with individual freedom, equally promote cultivation and population. Great improvements may take place in the state of society, but I do not see how the present form, or system, can be radically & essentially changed, without a danger of relapsing again into barbarism.[21]

Their disagreement was equally fundamental. Malthus saw human beings as short-sighted and selfish creatures who ran out of control without forces (natural or man-made) to guide them. Godwin never wavered in his belief that humanity could better itself through reason and compassion.

Less cordial were Godwin's letters to James Mackintosh a few months later. Mackintosh had been a prominent radical, author of one of the best known replies to Burke, the pamphlet *Vindicae Gallicae* (1791). A lawyer, in early 1799 he was scheduled to give a series of lectures at Lincoln's Inn on 'the Law of Nature and Nations' and sent the preliminary *Discourse* to Godwin. The philosopher was horrified. Godwin was probably aware that Mackintosh had gradually walked back from the hotly pro-revolutionary position he had occupied a few years earlier but the vehemence of Mackintosh's attack on radical culture in the *Discourse* left him reeling. In their correspondence, Mackintosh claimed that he was critical of doctrines, not people, yet (without naming names) the *Discourse* excoriates 'promulgators of absurd and monstrous systems' and 'sophists swelled with insolent conceit'.[22] Godwin demanded to know exactly who the lawyer meant by this, suspecting that Mackintosh's invective was aimed at him personally. The lawyer denied that Godwin was his target, reiterating his friendship and respect over several letters, but also implying that he saw the whole affair as an intellectual sparring match:

> With respect to you personally I could never mean to say anything unkind or disrespectful – I had always highly esteemed both your acuteness & benevolence. – You published opinions which you believed to be true & most Salutary but which I had from the first thought mistakes of a most dangerous tendency. – You did your duty in making public your opinions. I do mine by attempting to refute them …[23]

Godwin took the matter personally. He did not criticise Mackintosh for his apostasy, he respected the right to change one's mind, but he was obviously hurt by the abusiveness of the lawyer's rhetoric. Nevertheless, Godwin attended some of the lectures in person. The philosopher felt increasingly isolated. He fell out with Basil Montagu, amidst rumours that the younger man had joined the chorus of Godwin's critics (a charge Montagu only evasively denied). Holcroft took his family to the continent in July 1799, in a bid to escape the reactionary press, and would not return for three years. A letter to an unknown friend reveals Godwin's state of mind:

> I am on the point of losing Holcroft, whom I am not at all inclined to compare with you; if I lose you too, I shall have no instructor, no adviser, no pilot, but, trusted to my own devices, shall be left to make every day blunders as egregious as I am told I made in the publication of the Memoirs, where I consulted neither.[24]

Around the same time that Holcroft left, the husband of Godwin's friend of some years Maria Reveley died suddenly. Reveley was a highly accomplished and intelligent woman, one of the few to ever impress Godwin's peer Jeremy Bentham (her late husband had designed Bentham's panopticon) and later a close friend of Godwin's daughter Mary. She and Godwin had a complicated relationship; Godwin believed that she was in love with him. He proposed marriage within a month of her husband's death, but his series of agonised letters (two in July, another in August, and a last-ditch attempt in November) had no effect.

Figure 3   John Opie's 1797 portrait of Wollstonecraft watched over
Godwin as he worked at the Polygon, and later at Skinner Street.

Throughout all this, Godwin continued to write. No longer needing a separate working space, he hung a portrait of Wollstonecraft above his desk in the study of the home they had rented together at the Polygon. His next project was another novel, a work of historical fantasy that explores ideas about family and responsibility. It took almost two years of his life: he put pen to paper a month after finishing the *Memoir* (on 31 December, 1797) and finished at the end of November 1799. *St Leon: A Tale of the Sixteenth Century* is by far Godwin's longest novel. No doubt drained by the upheavals within his circle of friends, the philosopher found the work an exhausting undertaking. He wrote to George Robinson (the publisher) in September 1799 to explain his delays saying that he 'might have completed it three times over by this time, had I been less scrupulous'. [25] Famously, when asked by Byron years later why he did not write another novel, Godwin replied that the effort would kill him. "'And what matter," said Lord Byron; "we should have another *St Leon*."'[26]

The novel is perhaps best known for its preface. Much like the introductions to his other fictional works, Godwin comments on some of the sources that inspired him, and makes the customary author's apology to the reader who does not find the work to their taste. In the preface to *St Leon*, however, the apology touches on Godwin's philosophical works:

> Some readers of my graver productions will perhaps, in perusing these little volumes, accuse me of inconsistency; the affections and charities of private life being every where in this publication a topic of the warmest eulogium, while in the Enquiry concerning Political Justice they seemed to be treated with no great degree of indulgence and favour. In answer to this objection, all I think it necessary to say on the present occasion is, that, for more than four years, I have been anxious for opportunity and leisure to modify some of the earlier chapters of that work in conformity to the sentiments inculcated in this. Not that I see cause to make any change respecting the principle of justice, or any thing else fundamental to the system there delivered; but that I apprehend domestic and private affections inseparable from the nature of man, and from what may be styled the culture of the heart, and am fully persuaded that they are not incompatible with a profound and active sense of justice...

To philosophers who had kept up with Godwin's work, this was only really a strengthening of the language used in the revised *Political Justice* and *The Enquirer*. Casual readers were somewhat more surprised. The novel won unlikely plaudits from the *Anti-Jacobin Review*, who commended Godwin's change of heart (it did not save the philosopher from a parody novel – *St Godwin* – that made a mocking apology for the absurdity of his doctrines).

The titular St Leon is entrusted with the Philosopher's Stone by a mysterious traveller, on the condition that he keep its existence a secret even from his wife and children. The stone grants its user unlimited wealth and eternal youth, but the protagonist resolves to use its power for philanthropy rather than merely gain. St Leon's wealth brings him suspicion and harassment wherever he goes, however, and the secret alienates him from his family. The novel's major themes are all ideas that were likely at the forefront of Godwin's mind at the end of the decade: St Leon's wife, Marguerite de Damville, is commonly taken as a portrait of Wollstonecraft (Holcroft certainly thought so) but the saintly Marguerite resembles Wollstonecraft only insomuch as Godwin aimed to depict them both as exemplary women. Marguerite's wisdom and patience temper St Leon's passion and recklessness, much as the philosopher contrasts Wollstonecraft's intuition with his own judgment, but direct parallels between them are few. Nevertheless, companionship and affection are explored throughout the novel with a complexity that defies any attempt to read the text as a straightforward celebration of the family. The novel also alludes to Godwin's persecution by the state-sponsored reactionary movement. For all his faults, St Leon attempts to do good for humanity – yet his actions are misconstrued and his motives questioned. Like the defendants of 1794, the protagonist is imprisoned for hypothetical crimes (he cannot have arrived at his money honestly, therefore he must be locked up while the crime is uncovered) and his home in Italy is destroyed in an attack that deliberately recalls the Priestley Riots of 1792. As a mob burns the family's villa, St Leon's friend the Marchese exclaims:

> ... no innocence, and no merit, could defend a man from the unrelenting antipathy of his fellows. He saw that there was a principle in the human mind destined to be eternally at war with improvement and science. No sooner did a man devote himself to the pursuit of discoveries which, if ascertained, would prove the highest benefit to his species, than his whole species became armed against him. ... He saw, in the transactions of that night, a pledge of the eternal triumph of ignorance over wisdom.[27]

The philosopher himself was not so pessimistic.

6

The Educator
1800–09

Godwin was not entirely bound to his desk in the two years he devoted to *St Leon*. In 1798 he spent a few weeks in Bath, then the great tourist resort (and marriage market) of middle- and upper-class England. He attracted the attention of fellow novelist Harriet Lee; after Godwin returned home the two enjoyed weeks of philosophical correspondence. Godwin proposed marriage, but Lee congenially rejected him, citing the differences in their religious beliefs (Lee was a pious member of the Church of England) and Godwin's status as a controversial figure. Ironically, Godwin would soon have cause to revise his thoughts on religion in the light of a new friendship.

The philosopher had first met Samuel Taylor Coleridge at a dinner held by Holcroft in 1794. Coleridge had not been impressed, telling Thelwall that Godwin 'talked futile sophisms in jejune language' and attacking *Political Justice* in his philosophical lectures.[1] Coleridge wrote many years later that he had only half-understood Godwin's work at the time, and that the fervour of his criticism had been more about his own ignorance than anything found in Godwin's ideas.[2] The two met again at the end of 1799 while Godwin was on an extended trip through the Home Counties visiting, among others, Charles James Fox and Sir Francis Burdett. Their reacquaintance was evidently successful for, when Godwin returned to London, Coleridge called at the Polygon (or otherwise engaged him) regularly until Coleridge left London in April 1800. Coleridge had gravitated from an orthodox Anglican upbringing to Unitarianism in his early twenties, in part influenced by the scholar William Frend.[3] Their discussions prompted Godwin to re-examine his own beliefs:

I ceased to regard the name of Atheist with the same complacency I had done for several preceding years, at the same time retaining the utmost repugnance of understanding for the idea of an intelligent Creator and Governor of the universe, which strikes my mind as the most irrational and ridiculous anthropomorphism. My theism, if such I may be permitted to call it, consists in a reverent and soothing contemplation of all that is beautiful, grand, or mysterious in the system of the universe ...[4]

Unitarianism, at its core, is a theological movement that denies the mainstream Christian doctrine of the Holy Trinity – something that remained an offence under English law until 1810. Unitarians consider Jesus to have been a great prophet, but not God Incarnate. Many Unitarians also reject ideas such as original sin or eternal damnation, concepts that Godwin was himself critical of. The position that Godwin describes in his thoughts above suggests a form of Pantheism, the belief that divinity is found in all things, though the philosopher's discussion of this in the unfinished *Genius of Christianity Unveiled* (written around 1835) describes a broader, only semi-religious, awe for nature in its totality. Godwin sees nature as a system of mutually supporting life underpinned by physical laws, something worthy of admiration but beyond our ability to fully understand. We can (and should) observe and record the operations of nature to better understand them, but the origins of the universe are beyond human comprehension. Godwin obviously rejects the idea of an intelligent creator, and possibly the idea of spirit or divinity more generally, but neither is he purely a materialist. The philosopher was gradually moving towards this position from his first acquaintance with Coleridge to his final years, as hinted in his subsequent writing on Greek myth (*The Pantheon*, 1806) and his unpublished essay 'Of Religion' (1818).

Coleridge's own religious views would change further over the years, abandoning Unitarianism around 1805 in favour of an increasingly complicated (but theoretically Trinitarian) theology influenced by Spinoza, Schelling and Kant. Godwin found Coleridge's conversation fascinating, and tolerated the younger man's high-handedness and inconsistency in return for their many discussions of philosophy, religion and language. Godwin considered Coleridge the last of his four 'oral instructors' alongside Fawcett, Holcroft and George Dyson.

Coleridge introduced Godwin to Charles Lamb, then a young clerk for the East India Company and occasional poet, but eventually to become one of the most highly regarded essayists of the period. Like Coleridge, Lamb was quickly converted from a critic of Godwin to a friend, writing to another recent acquaintance, Thomas Manning that Godwin was 'a well-behaved decent man':

> ... nothing very brilliant about him or imposing as you might suppose; quite another Guess sort of Gentleman from what your Anti Jacobins Christians imagine him–. I was well pleased to find he has neither horns nor claws, quite a tame creature I assure you.[5]

Lamb had strong Unitarian sympathies, and some of his writing before meeting Godwin suggests that, like many, Lamb thought that *Political Justice* had put reason in God's place.[6] There is a certain truth to this, as the first edition discusses reasoning and truth in the same language that Godwin's Dissenting forbears might have used to describe faith and revelation. Perhaps expecting a de-Christianising Robespierre, Lamb seems to have been disarmed by Godwin's placidity and dry humour: Lamb and his friend Charles Lloyd had been grotesqued in Gillray's 'New Morality' cartoon alongside Godwin; when Lamb grew argumentative at their first meeting, Godwin quietly asked him if he was the toad or the frog. Lamb's answer is not recorded, but since he and Godwin met again for breakfast the next day, he might have been amused.[7]

Godwin's third major new friend in these years was William Hazlitt. Hazlitt was over twenty years Godwin's junior but the two had much in common – both the sons of Dissenting ministers (Hazlitt's father had preached at Wisbech after the Godwins had left in 1758), who were educated at Dissenting Academies (by Andrew Kippis), but who ultimately rejected Christianity in adult life. Hazlitt first met Godwin as a student in 1794, probably through Holcroft, but the two began to meet regularly when Hazlitt returned to London in early 1799. Though Hazlitt was, at this time, training to become a painter under the tutelage of his elder brother, he harboured the ambition to write. He would develop into a formidable essayist and critic, and it was with Godwin's help that he would publish his first major work (*An Essay on the Principles of Human Action*) in 1805.

All three of Godwin's new friends seethed protectively at Mackintosh's lectures. Lamb called the lawyer Judas, though noted that at least the Biblical betrayer had been decent enough to hang himself.[8] Perhaps Mackintosh had felt some remorse: he had, after all, sent Godwin advance warning of his assault and was quick to insist that he meant the philosopher no ill will. Samuel Parr's very public defection in April 1800 was another matter entirely.

Parr had, as an Anglican minister renowned for his learning, been asked to give an Easter sermon before the Lord Mayor of London and the governors of the Royal Hospital. Like Mackintosh, Parr took the opportunity to denounce the 'New Philosophy' and laud the status quo. The idea of 'universal philanthropy' was dangerous, Parr argued, as it steered the efforts of virtuous people away from helping those closest to them. 'The community of mankind', Parr said, was a 'rhetorical ornament' and, while it was moral to help those in need regardless of differences in culture or religion, it required too great an effort for all but the most virtuous.[9] Parr argued that Christianity did not confuse compassion with justice – the proper object of our benevolence is the people that love us. Philanthropy, Parr implies, is best left to those who have the means to help the least fortunate without diluting what they provided to their nearest and dearest (i.e. men such as his audience).

Godwin heard about the sermon second-hand and went in search of an explanation. He called on 19 April, but Parr excused himself by saying he was on his way out. When Godwin tried to call again on the 24th, he was told that Parr was not in London. The philosopher wrote a proud but wounded letter requesting some justification for Parr's attack. Parr had not replied to his letter about Mackintosh some months earlier, nor to the copy of *St Leon* that Godwin had sent after it:

If however both my letter & my visits would have passed unnoticed, I am entitled to conclude that you have altered your mind respecting me. In that case, I should be glad you would answer to your own satisfaction, what crime I am chargeable with, now in 1800, of which I had not been guilty in 1794, when with so much kindness & zeal you sought my acquaintance.[10]

Parr wrote a substantial answer a few days later. The letter praised Mackintosh's high character and called Godwin's complaints offensive (he claimed to have lost the philosopher's earlier letter). He denied that he had ever sought Godwin's company, referring to his former politeness as merely a dutiful respect to the philosopher's intellect (this was disingenuous; Parr said in a letter of September 1794 that he was 'ambitious of [Godwin's] friendship').[11] He claimed to have read only the preface of *St Leon*, and felt no curiosity to proceed further. Parr wrote that he had been displeased by *The Enquirer*'s comments on religion, shocked by the *Memoir*, and claimed that Godwin's philosophy had been a pernicious influence on the character of 'two or three young men, whose talents I esteemed, and whose virtues I loved'.[12] The letter was clear that Parr did not wish to hear from the philosopher again. The philosopher began a reply regardless, but does not appear to have finished it. Godwin wrote that he felt 'the most pungent grief in witnessing your disgrace; but since it must be so, I am well satisfied to possess this evidence ...'[13] Parr returned his copy of *St Leon* in October, with a formal – third-person – note that sought to imply that he had not read it, though his family had. The matter might have ended there, much as it had with Mackintosh, but Parr published his sermon in early 1801 – including extensive notes (some five times the length of the sermon itself) that quoted Godwin repeatedly and made it explicit that the philosopher was the target of Parr's criticism. The notes reproduced a lengthy section of the preface to *St Leon*, commending Godwin's 'maturer reflection' and 'contrition' but declaring that this concession (Parr magnanimously refuses to call it such) undermines the entirety of Godwin's concept of justice.[14]

Godwin hit back with his own pamphlet a few months later. The *Reply to Parr* began with the complaint that its author had endured a torrent 'of ribaldry, invective and intolerance' since the popular climate had turned against the French Revolution and the cause of freedom.[15] Stressing how widely *Political Justice* was praised upon its first publication, Godwin asserts that the floodgates opened in mid-1797 – a trickle of 'two little skirmishing pamphlets' quickly becoming a flood of 'scurrilities' and 'vulgar contumelies' in the anti-Jacobin press, with Parr's sermon bringing up the rear.[16] The philosopher names many of the writers and works he feels have wronged him but specifically exempts Malthus and the *Essay* for what Godwin saw as that work's respectable, collegial spirit. The philosopher insists that he had done nothing more than advance peaceful ideas with intellectual humility:

I wrote my Enquiry Concerning Political Justice in the innocence of my heart. I sought no overt effects; I abhorred all tumult; I entered my protest against revolutions. Every impartial person who knows me, or has attentively considered my writings, will acknowledge that it is the fault of my character, rather to be too sceptical, than to incline too much to play the dogmatist. I was by no means assured of the truth of my own system. I wrote indeed with ardour; but I published with diffidence. I knew that my speculations had led me out of the beaten track; and I waited to be instructed by the comment of others as to the degree of value which should be stamped upon them. That comment in the first instance was highly flattering; yet I was not satisfied. I did not cease to revise, to reconsider, or to enquire.[17]

Godwin (quite reasonably) felt that his ideas had been misrepresented. He accused Mackintosh of calling him bloodthirsty and alleged that the lawyer had avoided naming him only to sidestep the boundaries of decency in his abuse. Of Parr, the philosopher is scathing: there is a rare note of contempt in how Godwin describes the tardiness of Parr's attack ('he has condescended to join a cry, after it had already become loud and numerous').[18] The rest of essay seeks to clarify and defend *Political Justice*, beginning with the philosopher's revised position on the domestic affections. Following Parr, Godwin quotes from the preface to *St Leon* ('though, from some cause, he [Parr] has not specified the book from which the quotation is taken').[19] The philosopher sees no reason why acknowledging the value of domestic affection should in any way jeopardise the rest of his treatise – if it is our duty to create as much good as we can, then doing good for those closest to us is frequently the most effective use of our time. Godwin argues that most of the actual differences between his position and Parr's are matters of emphasis: both agree that domestic benevolence is easy and universal benevolence is hard, but while Parr holds the position that benevolence outside our immediate circle should not be entered into without prudence, Godwin argues that it is *domestic* benevolence that stands in need of regulation (essentially, that we should not spoil our families while others stand in need). The philosopher goes on to clarify his use of the term 'perfectibility', 'what I would now wish to call, changing the term, without changing a particle of the meaning, the progressive nature of man, in knowledge, in virtuous propensities, and in social institutions'.[20] What follows is Godwin's most pointed statement about his own optimism. Normally conciliatory in reference to principled conservatism (he refers to it in *The Enquirer* as a reluctance to gamble existing achievements for new ones), the philosopher recognises in his opponents an irreconcilable difference in their understanding of basic human nature:

> I know that Dr Parr and Mr Mackintosh look with horror upon this doctrine of the progressive nature of man. They cling with all the fervours of affection, to the opinion that vices, the weaknesses and the follies which have hitherto existed in our species, will continue undiminished as long as the earth shall endure. I do not envy them their feelings. I love to contemplate the yet unexpanded powers and capabilities of our nature, and to believe that they will one day be unfolded to the infinite advantage and happiness of the inhabitants of the globe. Long habit has so trained me to bow to the manifestations of truth wherever I recognize them, that, if arguments were presented to me sufficient to establish the uncomfortable doctrine of my antagonists, I would weigh, I would revolve them, and I hope I should not fail to submit to their authority. But, if my own doctrine is an error, and if I am fated to die in it, I cannot afflict myself greatly with the apprehension of a mistake, which cheers my solitude, which I carry with me into crowds, and which adds somewhat to the pleasure and peace of every day of my existence.[21]

The *Reply* continues this theme in response to Malthus, observing that the economist's conclusions (that inequality and suffering are inevitable consequences of population growth) are easily turned to conservative ends; indeed, 'the advocates of old establishments and old abuses' – Godwin uses this phrase to describe Parr elsewhere in the essay – 'could not have found a doctrine, more to their hearts content, more effectual to shut out all reform and improvement for ever'.[22] Yet Godwin's answer to Malthus was good-natured, suggesting that their conversations in person had convinced him that they were colleagues in solving the problem of population rather than scholarly rivals. Godwin declared himself to be in agreement with the economist's central theory (that population multiplied until checked by the limits of subsistence) but argued that its conclusions could be overcome – implicitly that the gradual improvement of private judgment included the consideration of sustainable population growth. Unwisely, Godwin discussed how societies had historically taken steps to actively curb population growth, principally through exposing unwanted babies to the elements. Though the philosopher had only described (not advocated) such practices, his usual detractors leapt upon this as further evidence of his monstrous, Spartan, logic and Godwin felt the need to send an appalled letter to the *Monthly Magazine* to protest his misrepresentation.[23]

The *Reply to Parr* is learned, passionate and, at times, waspishly amusing. Responses were mixed, though many concurred that Godwin had been treated poorly by his critics. The reactionary press was undeterred, the *British Critic* asserting that the philosopher had got off lightly (as such controversial opinions would have seen him guillotined in France). The pamphlet definitely made an impact with Malthus, however. The economist called on Godwin when he was next in London a few months later. The second edition of the *Essay on Population* features a short chapter responding to Godwin's comments in the *Reply*, agreeing that it was possible for individuals to reason themselves out of procreating (carrying out a moral duty to not increase the population unsustainably) but declaring that 'Mr. Godwin's system of political justice' was not conducive to its wide adoption.[24]

In the midst of all these controversies Godwin continued to write. In concert with the ever-lengthening *St Leon*, Godwin had been working on another play. In one respect, the theatre represented the opportunity to make money – a successful play offered a source of continual revenue rather than a one-off payment (as he would usually earn for a novel). In another, perhaps more important, fashion the stage offered a wider audience for Godwin's ideas. *Caleb Williams* (by far the philosopher's greatest success) was by this time on its third edition in five years, and had no doubt reached many thousands of readers, but London's two patent theatres (Drury Lane and Covent Garden) sold in excess of 10,000 tickets a week between them.[25] A play could reach a wider spectrum of society than a novel, too, from the servants and sailors in the upper gallery to the fashionable ladies and gentlemen in the boxes – new novels were (relatively) expensive, and many avid readers relied on subscription libraries to feed their interests.[26]

Godwin's new play had been through several titles and, since finishing the initial draft, had been passed through several friends in search of feedback. Holcroft had read the play before departing for Europe, with

Godwin providing a set of guidelines for how his friend might phrase his usual punishing criticism (Holcroft ignored it). Godwin read Coleridge's verse tragedy *Osorio*, which bore a number of similarities to his own play. Sheridan, who owned Drury Lane, had offered to stage Godwin's piece after an early glance at the manuscript in April 1799, but nothing initially came of this. Godwin tried again, submitting it anonymously to George Colman at the Haymarket Theatre (who had adapted *Caleb Williams* for the stage as *The Iron Chest*, without the philosopher's input) only to have it rejected. Godwin spent the summer of 1800 in Ireland as the guest of the Irish MP John Philpot Curran, where he was able to meet Wollstonecraft's onetime pupil, Lady Mountcashell. On his return he tried Sheridan again, who passed him on to the great actor-manager of the Theatre Royal, John Phillip Kemble, who accepted the play – but quickly learned to regret it.

Antonio, or The Soldier's Return is a verse tragedy that draws on Elizabethan and Jacobean styles of drama. The titular protagonist returns home from the wars to find that his sister has married against his wishes, jilting his brave friend to whom she was betrothed. He kidnaps her in a bid to salvage what he perceives as his family's honour but is foiled by his sister's husband. The play concludes with Antonio murdering his sister rather than allowing her to remain married. At a time when the most successful plays leaned heavily on spectacle (parades, costumes, action), Godwin's piece relies on its poetry to make the drama. The play seems constructed to make the audience listen and think – as in any proper tragedy, each character has their own valid complaints against the others, and the play does its best not to distract from those arguments being heard. *Antonio* reflects Godwin's concerns about debate and rhetoric: each character is allowed to make their case, and their opponents a rebuttal, the play does not permit any one actor to sweep the audience along with them and dictate how the story will be received. For all this seems intellectually sound, it makes terrible theatre.

Kemble had reservations almost immediately but pestering from Godwin, and implicit orders from Sheridan, persuaded Kemble both to produce and take the lead role. The famous Sarah Siddons (who had been one of those who dropped Wollstonecraft after her marriage to Godwin) played Antonio's sister, Helena. Afraid that the play would receive brickbats just for having his name attached to it, Godwin asked the playwright John Tobin to pose as the author. The philosopher was gratingly confident, soliciting advice on what his share of the profits should be and planning out how he would spend the money (on more books, according to Lamb). Kemble twisted in an attempt to get out of the part, but to no avail. The play's sole performance (on 13 December 1800) was a disaster, the night captured memorably in a later essay by Lamb:

Great expectations were formed. A philosopher's first new play was a new era. The night arrived. I was favoured with a seat in an advantageous box, between the author and his friend M—. G. sate cheerful and confident. In his friend M.'s looks, who had perused the manuscript, I read some terror. Antonio in the person of John Philip Kemble at length appeared, starched out in a ruff which no one could dispute, and in most irreproachable mustachios. John always dressed most provokingly correct on these occasions. The first act swept by, solemn and silent. It went off, as G. assured M., exactly as the opening act of a piece – the protasis – should do. The cue of the spectators was to be mute. ... The second act (as in duty bound) rose a little in interest; but still John kept his forces under – in policy, as G. would have it – and the audience were most complacently attentive. The protasis, in fact, was scarcely unfolded. The interest would warm in the next act, against which a special incident was provided. M. wiped his cheek, flushed with a friendly perspiration – 'tis M.'s way of showing his zeal – 'from every pore of him a perfume falls –'. I honour it above Alexander's. He had once or twice during this act joined his palms in a feeble endeavour to elicit a sound – they emitted a solitary noise without an echo – there was no deep to answer to his deep. G. repeatedly begged him to be quiet. ... A challenge was held forth upon the stage, and there was promise of a fight. The pit roused themselves on this extraordinary occasion, and, as their manner is, seemed disposed to make a ring, – when suddenly Antonio, who was the challenged, turning the tables on the hot challenger, Don Gusman (who by the way should have had his sister) baulks his humour, and the pit's reasonable expectation at the same time, with some speeches out of the new philosophy against duelling. The audience were here fairly caught – their courage was up, and on the alert – a few blows, ding dong, as R—s the dramatist afterwards expressed it to me, might have done the business – when their most exquisite moral sense was suddenly called in to assist in the mortifying negation of their own pleasure. They could not applaud, for disappointment; they would not condemn, for morality's sake. The interest stood stone still; and John's manner was not at all calculated to unpetrify it. It was Christmas time, and the atmosphere furnished some pretext for asthmatic affections. One began to cough – his neighbour sympathised with him – till a cough became epidemical.[27]

Reviews were universally negative. The *London Chronicle*, attempting some consolation, suggested that it would make a reasonable closet drama (i.e. a play to be read, not performed). Godwin enlisted Lamb's help in revising the play once more and published it on 23 December. The reviews were no better. The philosopher was not discouraged. At the suggestion of Coleridge, he quickly began work on a new tragedy, *Abbas, King of Persia*. He finished the first draft by April 1801 and sent the manuscript off to his friend in the Lake District. Coleridge dragged his feet in replying. He eventually confessed that his first round of criticism had been irreverent and hurtful, and wrote that he had held off returning the play to Godwin until he had revised his observations. The notes Coleridge eventually dispatched were still far from gentle, recommending an extensive rewrite and identifying every point in the play the poet considered clichéd, flat, or vulgar. Godwin took his friend's criticism seriously, returning to the play directly and continuing to revise the play even after he had submitted it to Thomas Harris at Covent Garden at the end of August. This proved unsuccessful and the play was submitted anonymously to Drury Lane for consideration in September. *Abbas* shows Godwin making certain concessions to the theatre arts: the play makes use of spectacle, but also criticises it. From his letters to Coleridge it is clear that the use of such techniques troubled him, that he feared pandering to the audience's expectations would damage the play as a literary creation. The play was potentially controversial, using the Sunni/ Shi'a schism to discuss religious conflict in a way that had obvious implications for Protestant/Catholic strife in Ireland. In other aspects, the play reflected the longstanding political conflict between the King (a steadfast conservative) and the Prince of Wales (no radical, but an ally of Fox and Sheridan). Sadly for Godwin, his concerns were academic: *Abbas* was quickly rejected by both Covent Garden and Drury Lane. He complained to Kemble. Over-stepping the mark in his assessment of his own talent as a dramatist ('I think it scarcely fair that I should come before them as an unknown novice…'), he received a brusque reply. Godwin attempted to badger Kemble into accepting the play, begging for his input on how to improve it. He wrote to Sheridan in the hope that the MP would lean on his employee. It had no obvious effect. Kemble's replies were irate rather than hostile, but his rejection was emphatic, repeating several times that he would reappraise the work if it was revised, but not until then. This at least gave Godwin pause, and he would not return to dramatic writing until a few years had passed; after the first draft of *Abbas* he turned to writing the *Reply to Parr*. Also in the offing was a proposed biography of Chaucer, but he was unable to attend to that seriously until the end of the year. Events that year would lead to a change in the philosopher's living arrangements, however, and a new focus for his ideas.

Godwin's diary records 'Meet Mrs Clairmont' on 5 May 1801. Mary Jane Clairmont was a neighbour at the Polygon with children of a similar age to Godwin's own. He visited her often, sometimes with the children and sometimes without. The diary implies that they became lovers in July (it reads 'tea Clairmonts X') but kept matters confidential. Much of what we know about Mary Jane is second hand. She did not write daily notes to Godwin, as Wollstonecraft had, and some of the letters she did write to him are lost. Although an author in her own right, none of her works have the vibrantly personal touch that we see in the rest of the family's writing. She kept her past private. She spent some of her childhood in France and fled to Spain during the revolution. She told her children that their father had been a Swiss merchant known as Karl Gaulis (which he later Anglicised to 'Clairmont') who had died in Hamburg in 1798. Twentieth century research casts some doubt on this – Gaulis appears to have died in Silesia in 1796, making it unlikely that he was the father of Mary's daughter Jane (born April 1798). In 2011, genealogist Vicki Parslow Stafford was able to identify that Jane was the illegitimate daughter of Sir John Lethbridge (a West Country landowner), who provided occasional financial support for his daughter until 1814.[28] Godwin knew she was not a widow, as she claimed to others (she had been born Mary Vial, and the couple were married under that name in 1802).[29] Many of the stories about their courtship are apocryphal, dating from after the death of both, but legend has it that Clairmont was the hunter: she flattered the philosopher extravagantly and engineered opportunities for him to overhear her pining for him. Godwin's vanity and Clairmont's later reputation for dishonesty give credence to the stories, but our portrait of Clairmont owes much to unflattering sources – Lamb found their affair ridiculous (he wrote in September 1801, 'the Professor is grown quite juvenile') and rarely missed the opportunity to mock her in his letters. Her soon-to-be stepdaughter, the future Mary Shelley, would come to hate her.

In October 1801, Clairmont found herself pregnant with Godwin's child. The couple were married on 21 December – twice. Clairmont and Godwin held a small ceremony in Shoreditch in the morning, with Marshall (again) as witness, before proceeding to a second wedding in Whitechapel the same day. The first records the marriage of Mary Clairmont, widow; the second, Mary Vial, spinster. The exact reason for the second wedding is unclear, but biographers have speculated that Clairmont sought a degree of insurance to prevent the marriage being struck down if the false statement of the first wedding (i.e. that she was a widow) was ever uncovered. Godwin did not note the second occasion in his diary. It is unclear as to when the baby was born, the philosopher does not record it in his diary, but the child (a boy, William) did not survive long: Godwin marks his death on 4 June. Clairmont was soon pregnant again and, on 28 March 1803, delivered another baby boy – William Godwin Junior. The Godwins were now an extensive clan: William, Mary Jane, Fanny (now nine), Mary Jane's son Charles (seven), Mary (five), Jane (later called Claire, then aged four) and newborn William Junior.

The greatly expanded family was desperately short of money. The failure of *Antonio* had already driven Godwin to write what he openly called 'begging letters' to his richer friends.[30] He was finding it harder to find work. Godwin's regular publisher George Robinson died in 1801. Clairmont spoke excellent French and German and turned this into translation work, while preparing children's books for the publisher Benjamin Tabart. Inspired by Thomas Tyrwhitt's 1798 edition of the *Canterbury Tales*, Godwin proposed a biography of Chaucer to the up-and-coming publisher Richard Phillips. Phillips offered a contract within days, perhaps thanks to an antiquarian interest of his own (Phillips accompanied Godwin on a trip to visit the 'Chaucer house' at Woodstock; the philosopher wrote to Clairmont of how dull the publisher was on his own).[31]

More than simply a biography, the *Life of Chaucer* is a wide-ranging cultural history of fourteenth-century England. The philosopher researched deeply, with 'almost daily attendance at the British Museum' and venturing out of London to consult records in the Bodleian Library and the Chaucer manuscripts held at Gonville and Caius College, Cambridge.[32] Godwin sought to explore the world that had made the poet, and throughout the work stresses the depth of feeling and sentiment in Chaucer's character to explain the quality and timelessness of his poetry. The work contains a close reading of Chaucer's lesser-known works, searching for insight into the character of the poet and placing him in context alongside the other greats of medieval verse. The philosopher worked on his history doggedly for two whole years. The *Life of Chaucer* is a mammoth work, and Godwin's preface implies that the philosopher was reined in by his publisher before he considered the book complete. It is best known for its iconic statement about literature and truth: commending Chaucer's decision to abandon the legal profession, Godwin opined that the sophistry that the law required would sit uneasily with literary genius.

Above all, the poet, whose judgment should be clear, whose feelings should be uniform and sound, whose sense should be alive to every impression and hardened to none, who is the legislator of generations and the moral instructor of the world, ought never to have been a practising lawyer, or ought speedily to have quitted so dangerous an engagement.[33]

The job of the literary artist was to keep a mind open to new experiences and to grow the imagination. Godwin worked on the *Life of Chaucer* alongside *Bible Stories* for Tabart. The preface of the latter expands upon the hints expressed in the history – the development of the imagination is not only the domain of literary genius, but an essential part of the human mind.

Imagination is the ground-plot upon which the edifice of a sound morality must be erected. Without imagination we may have a certain cold and arid circle of principles, but we cannot have sentiments: we may learn by rote a catalogue of rules, and repeat our lesson with the exactness of a parrot, or play over our tricks with the docility of a monkey; but we can neither ourselves love, nor be fitted to excite the love of others.[34]

Godwin claimed that contemporary children's books gave nothing to the soul, perhaps teaching 'practical' lessons about the world, or simply recommending obedience and piety, but not encouraging young people to think about anything beyond the world immediately around them. The intellectual and moral improvement of humanity – the central theme of all Godwin's philosophical works – requires that people be able to see beyond 'things as they are'. Implicit in all of Godwin's writing is the sense that a better world must be imagined before it can become possible. More essentially, however, Godwin argues that we cannot develop the capacity for critical moral reason without the ability to imagine what others feel (i.e. empathy or sympathy). Godwin had been edging towards a theory of how to develop this ever since he published his *Account of the Seminary* in 1783. The answer lay in reading. Continuing the line of thought he had advanced in *The Enquirer*, Godwin argued here that reading was vital to allow people the experience of imagining things that we cannot see, be they the thoughts of other people or ideas that do not yet exist.

In the spring of 1804, Godwin began work on his third major novel: *Fleetwood; or, the New Man of Feeling*. In *Fleetwood*, the philosopher took on Rousseau. *Fleetwood* is a novel about education, but more precisely it is a novel about the relationships between a learner and his mentors and how a certain kind of education leaves an individual ill-equipped to become a mentor themselves. Casimir Fleetwood's early education is one of indulgence. As a boy he is allowed to roam freely and explore the natural world. What formal education Casimir is given comes from a private tutor whom he finds ridiculous, and no greater scholarship is expected from him than that which he chooses to put his mind to. We can easily draw comparisons between this and Emile's semi-pastoral education, but Godwin read Rousseau closely – Fleetwood's narrative of his own early education is closer to the 'received' account of Rousseau's system put forward by period commentators. Fleetwood's real education comes at the hands of his mentors who, like Rousseau's preceptor, provide experiential moral lessons that shape the way he sees the world. Albeit with the best of intentions, Fleetwood's mentors manipulate him emotionally (winning his confidence with illiberal means, as *The Enquirer* put it) in order to make him receptive to the teachings they wish to impart. Fleetwood grows into an adult who knows how to feel, but not how to reason.

Fleetwood is, in style, a confession narrative. As in Godwin's other novels the philosopher uses the first person to convey the protagonist's emotional turmoil, here culminating in a bizarre and gothic nervous breakdown. Indeed, at various points in the novel we see hints of the philosopher's sense of the strange or absurd. Where *Fleetwood* differed from the philosopher's previous works was in Godwin's assertion (in the preface) that his narrator was a normal man, and that 'at least one half of the Englishmen now existing, who are of the same rank of life as my hero', had experienced similar.[35] The philosopher goes on to imply that his protagonist's ultimate reaction to these mundane events is exceptional but, predictably, Godwin's critics took it as an attempt to defame Englishmen everywhere. The *Anti-Jacobin Review* descended into an ugly tirade against the late Wollstonecraft (though it must be said that Godwin had mischievously named the novel's only genuine villain after the magazine's editor). More seriously, the novel caused a breach with Holcroft. Out of the blue, he sent a confused letter to Godwin:

I write to inform you that instead of seeing you at dinner tomorrow I desire to never see you more, being determined never to have *any* further intercourse with you of *any* kind.

T. Holcroft

Feb. 28, 1785.
P.S. *I* shall behave as becomes an honest and honourable man who remembers not only what is due to others but himself. There are indelible injuries that will not endure to be mentioned: such is the one you have committed on the man who would have *died* to serve you.[36]

Godwin was mystified and had to ask Clairmont (who had seen Holcroft that day) what offence he had given. *Fleetwood*'s Mr Scarborough to some extent represents the opposite extreme to the protagonist's Rousseauvian upbringing: drilling his son relentlessly, and always requiring perfection, the son falls into a spiral of depression and dies. Holcroft's own son had committed suicide in 1789, and he read Scarborough as an indictment of his parenting. Ironically, the philosopher had partly based the character on himself. He wrote to Marshall that Scarborough recalled his own failure as a mentor to Tom Cooper, and that there was no connection to Holcroft at all (he reported that he had solicited the opinions of at least twenty others, of whom none had seen any parallel with Holcroft). Godwin made some effort to explain matters to his friend, but to no avail. He wrote to Holcroft on 3 March that he would think of him as a dear friend who had died, rather than remember his abrupt and irrational desertion. They would not speak as friends for four years.

The critical response to *Fleetwood* was relatively lukewarm, and sales did not approach those of *Caleb Williams* or *St Leon* (Phillips printed nearly two thousand copies in his first run – a statement of remarkable confidence in Godwin's 'draw' as a novelist – but a second printing was not ordered until the copyright changed hands more than twenty-five years later). It perhaps became clear that literature was not an effective method of supporting a large family. Godwin proposed a comprehensive history of England to Phillips and began work on it shortly after *Fleetwood* was published. It was never completed. Though we are not party to whatever discussions the couple had, Godwin's biographers have assumed that it was Clairmont that proposed the family go into publishing for themselves. Mary Jane had worked on the editorial side of children's publishing for some years now, and probably had a solid understanding of what the business required. Godwin borrowed more money from the (now dying) Wedgwood, ostensibly to rectify his cash-flow problems, and rented a house and shop on Hanway Street, allowing them to retail books directly. Godwin would write, Clairmont would prepare the work for printing, and an employee by the name of Thomas Hodgkins would manage the shop. As with *Bible Stories*, Godwin was concerned that his name would attract bad press, perhaps dooming the business from the start. Their initial solution was to establish the venture in Hodgkins's name (as the 'Juvenile Library'), and to publish Godwin's writing under a series of pseudonyms. Godwin also approached Lamb to write for them.

Children's publishing combined Godwin's financial needs with his philosophical ones. The market for children's books was not necessarily a lucrative one, but it was consistent. Schools placed large orders and demand was perennial, Godwin could attract investors with projected returns rather than merely asking his friends for credit. More importantly, children's publishing allowed Godwin to put his educational philosophy into practice. The philosopher could take his ideas to the next generation of readers. He could even claim that his theories gave the proposed Juvenile Library a distinctive place in the market – if other children's authors were offering mundane stories, he would provide fantastic ones; where other children's authors would provide role models for children, he would encourage them to question who they wanted to be.

The books the Juvenile Library published in its first year exemplified this. Written under the name 'Edward Baldwin', *Fables, Ancient and Modern* was Godwin's adaptation of Aesop – a collection of short tales, with each offering some lesson about morality or self-knowledge. Where Godwin's *Fables* differed was in the nature of the lesson. Eighteenth-century versions of Aesop usually featured an explicit 'moral'; Samuel Croxall's 1722 *Fables of Aesop* (which Godwin drew on for his edition) sometimes adds a moral three or four times as long as the fable itself. Godwin's fables offer no explicit moral at all. While the inference we are supposed to draw from some stories is clear, the philosopher rarely seeks to dictate it. More often, the philosopher engages the reader to ask what they might have done in the protagonist's position. Most interestingly, Godwin sometimes adjusts the details of well-known fables so as to open them up for debate. The fable of the farmer and the viper (in Godwin, 'The Good-Natured Man and the Adder') is supposedly the origin of the phrase 'to nurse a snake in one's bosom' and is commonly given the moral that some individuals are never worthy of beneficence, or that it is in the nature of some to always do harm. Croxall criticises the farmer in this example for showing benevolence to an improper object. By contrast, Godwin has a neighbour (who has previously benefitted from the farmer's generosity) step in to save his protagonist. The philosopher ends by seeming to impose a reading on the fable, before undermining it with a note of scepticism about the story as a whole:

The good-natured man learned a wise lesson from this adventure: he saw how much mischief he had nearly brought upon himself by a kindness that paid no attention to the different qualities of living creatures; but then he saw that the life of his child had been saved by a person, to whom he had once acted generously, without acting imprudently.

The only thing that puzzles me in this story is the behaviour of the adder. It is contrary to the nature of all animals; for I have found it almost an universal rule, that no creature will harm you, if you have not first done that creature harm.[37]

The authorial voice in the *Fables* is affectionate and informal, as if the stories were told to children at their father's knee. Godwin's son Charles (then nine) is even addressed in the text. Some years earlier Coleridge had written to Southey of the 'cadaverous Silence of Godwin's children', which some have taken to indicate that the philosopher was a strict or distant father, but this does not seem to tally with the obvious warmth of Godwin as a children's author.[38]

The second publication of 1805 was even less traditional. *The Looking Glass* is a biography for children, the life story of Godwin's friend and illustrator William Mulready (at the time, still a teenager himself). Rather than presenting a finished life of great deeds, Godwin (writing as 'Theophilus Marcliffe') tells how Mulready's childhood shaped him into a dedicated and hardworking artist. Although the work celebrates its subject's determination and self-reliance, the story does not diminish the support Mulready received from parents and mentors on his journey. The artist is – realistically – shown to be a product of both nature and nurture, in contrast to fictional children's role models who succeeded through innate reserves of selflessness, industry, or wisdom. The book claims no such heroic qualities for its subject, attributing his success to a simple love for his vocation – which, as the title implies, is a virtue that the reader can look for within themselves.

The Juvenile Library struggled from the beginning. Perhaps not fully understanding the undertaking before him Godwin had only borrowed £100 from Wedgwood, money which quickly disappeared in the renting and outfitting of the shop. The work they published was good, many remaining in print long after the company went out of business and some still regarded as classics of children's literature: it was the Juvenile Library that first published Charles and Mary Lamb's *Tales from Shakespeare* (1807), and the first translation of Johann Wyss's *Swiss Family Robinson* (by Mary Jane Clairmont, 1814). Godwin's pseudonyms were apparently successful, his books receiving favourable notices in conservative journals. Wedgwood died in July 1805, leaving Godwin without a reliable financial backer. The philosopher borrowed heavily to keep the shop afloat, but also used his own (still good) credit to help those in greater need – letters show that around this time Godwin borrowed money to bail his friend, the scientist William Nicholson, who had been imprisoned for debt. The philosopher's finances very quickly became a tangled mess of debts both small and large. In the summer of 1807 both family and business moved to new premises in Skinner Street, thanks to a loan from Curran. It was not a desirable location, only a short distance from the Smithfield meat market and a stone's throw from the Fleet prison, but it was a better shop front than Hanway Street and provided more living space than the Polygon. The building had stood empty before the Godwin's moved in; its ownership was unclear. The ambiguity must have amused Godwin – he had always argued that property could only really belong to those who most needed it – and within a year he had decided to exploit the situation by refusing to pay rent until the 'rightful owners' were identified. The philosopher was taking a gamble, but it would be nearly ten years before any putative landlord was able to call his bluff. At some point in 1807 it became apparent that Hodgkins was taking money directly out of the business, possibly stealing stock or taking shop revenue for himself. Exactly what happened is unclear, but in August Godwin's diary records him changing the locks at Skinner Street and calling a constable in reference to '3 Hodgkinses'. Hodgkins was dismissed and the business re-established in Clairmont's name, as 'M. J. Godwin and Company', though retaining the Juvenile Library title. By the summer of 1808, however, the shop was in serious trouble – Godwin was convinced he would soon find himself in debtor's prison. With the help of Johnson and Marshall, Godwin attempted to raise money through public subscription. The appeal went out to the Whig party grandees, championed by Lord Holland (nephew of Charles James Fox) and the Earl of Lauderdale (then a radical peer), and receiving contributions from both the political and publishing worlds. It was enough to save the business, but it did not clear Godwin's debts or prevent him from accruing new ones.

Godwin's work rate in these years is impressive. In 1806 alone, the philosopher authored two substantial histories for children (*The History of England* and *The Life of Lady Jane Grey*), a book of Classical myths (*The Pantheon*), and another play (*Faulkener*, which would be performed the following year). Of these, only the drama was published under the philosopher's real name, allowing the philosopher to retreat from the (frequently hostile) spotlight. Political fortunes were changing too: Pitt had died in January 1806 and Grenville, seeking to form the strongest government possible, had formed a coalition that embraced both reformers and conservatives. Fox was foreign secretary, Erskine Lord Chancellor, Sheridan was Treasurer of the Navy. The *Anti-Jacobin*'s patron, George Canning, sat on the backbenches. The 'Ministry of All the Talents' did not last long – Fox died in September and the coalition broke up in March 1807 – but it is remembered principally as the government that brought about the abolition of the slave trade in the British Empire. As the subscription had demonstrated, Godwin's name still carried weight in political circles. It became clear that the philosopher's reputation was international when former US Vice President Aaron Burr paid a call in October 1808 and became a regular fixture at Skinner Street for the rest of his time in London (Burr considered himself a disciple of both Godwin and Wollstonecraft, but Godwin's later letters imply that the philosopher did not agree).

The failing business contributed to a decline in Godwin's health. From late 1807 the diary records three or four day periods of 'deliquium', at least once a year, for the next five years (and three outbreaks in 1814). It is not clear what this affliction was; the term describes a fainting fit, and Godwin described his attacks to a physician in May 1808:

> ... each fit (of perfect insensibility) lasted about a minute. Air was of no service to repel at fit, but hartshorn smelled to, or a draught of hartshorn and water, seemed to drive them off, particularly in the last days of an attack. If seized standing, I have fallen on the ground, and I have repeatedly had the fits in bed. ... in every instance each single fit seemed to find me and leave me in perfect health ... The approach of the fit is not painful, but is rather entitled to the name of pleasure, a gentle fading away of the senses; nor is the recovery painful, unless I am teased in it by persons about me.[39]

The symptoms have been described as episodes of catalepsy. The philosopher reported that the condition had affected him since his twenties, but the diary's evidence makes it apparent that between 1807 and 1814 Godwin was more frequently affected than at any other point in his life. If the ailment was in part psychological, then the sustained stress of being both writer and publisher would have obviously contributed to the problem.

On 19 March 1809 the philosopher was summoned to Holcroft's bedside. His friend was dying. When Godwin arrived, Holcroft was overcome with emotion. He pressed his hand to his chest and said, 'My dear, dear friend'. Godwin visited him every day until Holcroft's death on the 23rd, though the playwright was too weak to hold a conversation.[40] Godwin and Marshall organised a subscription to help Holcroft's wife and children.

Hazlitt undertook a biography, beginning from the narrative Holcroft had dictated from his deathbed. Hazlitt made extensive use of Holcroft's diary and letters, which he planned to publish separately, much to Godwin's consternation. In early 1810 he wrote a concerned letter to Holcroft's widow, Louisa. The controversy over the philosopher's memoir of Wollstonecraft had scarred him:

> It is one thing for a man to write a journal, and another for that journal to be given to the public. I am sure Mr Holcroft would never have consented to this. I have always entertained the highest antipathy to this violation of the confidence between man and man, that every idle word, every thoughtless jest I make at another's expense, shall be carried home by the hearer, put in writing, and afterwards printed. This part will cause fifty persons at least, who lived on friendly terms with Mr Holcroft, to execrate his memory. It will make you many bitter enemies, who will rejoice in your ruin, and be transported to see you sunk in the last distress. Many parts are actionable.[41]

Many have taken this (and later letters) to indicate that Godwin had reconsidered his views on sincerity. Relating the unvarnished truth about the dead had proved explosive for the living. Equally, the deceased's achievements could be obscured by a controversial life. Yet we should be wary of inferring such a fundamental challenge to Godwin's philosophical principles based on an unguarded comment, for precisely the reasons that he identifies in the letter.

> Two or three detestable stories (lies, I can swear) are told of Mrs Siddons; and Miss Smith, the actress, is quoted as the authority; that is, Miss Smith, as other people do, who are desirous of amusing their company, told these stories as she heard them, borne out with a sort of saw, 'You have them as cheap as I.' The first meeting of Emma Smith and Mr Holcroft occurs, and he sets her down, and Mr Hazlitt prints her, as a young woman of no talents; I believe Mr Holcroft altered his opinion on that subject.[42]

We have a duty to tell the truth that we know, but also to speak the truth responsibly. If the truth we know is incomplete (perhaps lacking context) then we may do potentially more harm than good. The rhetoric of *Political Justice*, particularly in its first edition, implied that the philosopher was untroubled by this (universal sincerity would wipe out falsehood and ambiguity) but even in 1793 Godwin recognised that there were good and bad ways to deliver the truth. *Political Justice* uses the example of delivering bad news to someone on their deathbed, arguing that, 'in reality there is a mode in which under such circumstances truth may safely be communicated; and, if it be not thus done, there is perpetual danger that it may be done in a blunter way'.[43] The duty to speak the truth remains absolute, but it must be done wisely. The revised editions of *Political Justice* complicate this further by acknowledging the difficulty of identifying objective truth at all. Arguably, Godwin saw the diary as the publication of an incomplete truth – he raised no objections to what Hazlitt had written *about* Holcroft – that could only damage the playwright's memory. In a series of (probably ill-tempered) meetings between Godwin, Hazlitt, Louisa Holcroft and others, Godwin and Hazlitt seem to have hammered out which parts of the diary were safe to include and which would only cause strife. The letter above indicates that Godwin was most concerned by stories the diary reported second hand. Such elements reflected more on the teller and the subject (rather than Holcroft) which had the potential to be legally problematic, but from a philosophical point of view their excision is consistent with a commitment to accuracy over transparency. Godwin was certain that some of the stories reported in the diary were untrue – while it might have been honest to note that Holcroft had heard them, the ethics of repeating them were questionable. Hazlitt's *Memoirs of the Late Thomas Holcroft* were not published until 1816, and raised no memorable controversy. Perhaps Godwin's editing had been effective, or perhaps the intervening years made Holcroft's opinions more a historical curiosity than anything to sue over. Most likely, Holcroft's notorious outspokenness in life had left no one surprised by the details in his memoirs. Everything that was controversial about Holcroft (his politics, his atheism, his mercurial temper) was already common knowledge.

A few months after Holcroft's death, Godwin's mother passed away at the age of 87. The son travelled to Norfolk for the funeral. After the service, he wrote a sad and probably heartfelt letter to Clairmont:

While my mother lived, I always felt to a certain degree as if I had
somebody who was my superior, and who exercised a mysterious
protection over me. I belonged to something – I hung to something
– there is nothing that has so much reverence and religion in it as
affection to parents. The knot is now severed, and I am, for the first
time, at more than fifty years of age, alone. You shall now be my mother;
you have in many instances been my protector and my guide ...[44]

Godwin and Clairmont's relationship was volatile. She harangued him
when she was unhappy and sulked when she did not get her way. She
lied to his friends as a matter of habit, making up stories to cover his
absences or inability to take callers. He remonstrated with her patiently
as often as he could – when his anger showed she was liable to walk
out until he apologised (when he fully lost his temper with her in 1811,
she moved out of the house for several weeks). Clairmont was under
the same strain as Godwin in running the Juvenile Library and, where
the philosopher put definite boundaries on his space and time (he was
usually writing upstairs during the day, if not out paying calls), Mary Jane
was usually surrounded by children, customers, or Godwin's friends and
disciples. In their rooms above, the philosopher's portrait of Wollstone-
craft was mounted prominently in the study, a constant reminder that
her husband's friends considered her a poor substitute for the author of
the *Vindication*. Godwin always defended her, browbeating the likes of
Holcroft or Coleridge into apologising for their rudeness to her. In the
chaos that was no doubt possible at Skinner Street, she probably appre-
ciated his calm. His letters acknowledge that he relied heavily on her
support. They learned how to live with each other.

7

The Father
1810–19

The Juvenile Library was, for much of its life, a troubled business. Since late 1809, Francis Place (the former LCS chair and future Chartist, a self-made man with a successful tailoring company) had worked with Godwin to put the family's business on a sound footing. The exact order of events is unclear but in early 1810 Godwin was calling on Place as well as the financier John Lambert and perhaps, with their advice, going through the Juvenile Library's accounts in search of a solution to the company's woes. Place estimated that, deducting the cost of the Library's liabilities from the value of its assets, the business had a net worth of £3,000. This was, relatively speaking, good news: with a substantial injection of capital, the business could become sustainably profitable. Place went in search of a backer and made the acquaintance of a wealthy young man called Elton Hammond, who was eager to use his fortune to help Godwin after having read what *Political Justice* had to say about property. Through much of 1811 Godwin and Place met weekly, perhaps trying to organise investors and guarantors for the business. Place, Lambert and Hammond all made donations and Place organised further monies through loans. Altogether their efforts raised £3,000, the amount Place believed would set the business on its feet. To the businessman's surprise and dismay, the funds quickly evaporated.

It is most likely that the money disappeared into Godwin's complicated network of creditors. Both family and business had survived up to this point through loans, borrowing money to make repayments of debts they already owed – Godwin's papers show nearly £1,000 of repayments due in the first quarter of 1811 alone. The threat of debtor's prison probably forced Godwin to use Place, Lambert and Hammond's money to clear existing debts rather than invest in the business as intended.

Place had his doubts, however. An instinctively frugal man, Place had forced himself to overcome a lifelong distaste for borrowing when he had gone into business for himself. He could only imagine that the money had been somehow wasted (he referred to Clairmont as an 'infernal devil' and wished Godwin a more 'prudent' wife) and believed Godwin to have presented him with false accounts in order to attract investment.[1] This seems unlikely: the family lived as sparsely as seven people under the same roof can be expected to. Another backer, Horace Smith, some years later described them as living in 'an almost primitive simplicity'.[2] Godwin ate little meat, believing that it contributed to his ill health, and drank even less (occasions when Godwin drank rum are recorded in the diary in Latin – it was the philosopher's habit to use other languages to note things he found embarrassing or distasteful). Nor was calculated deception really a part of Godwin's character. His pseudonyms were an open secret; he readily sent copies of his children's books to well-wishers, and a spy's report from 1813 indicates that the government were fully aware – and apparently unconcerned – that the philosopher was writing and selling books for children. Years of abuse had made him cautious and evasive; he had learned the hard way that ambiguity was often safer than transparency, but he was never comfortable with outright lies. Surviving in business had taught him to flatter, to promise more than he could deliver, and to beg if necessary. He had come to resemble the caricature of a shopkeeper he presented in *The Enquirer*, 'so much in the habit of exhibiting a bended body, that he scarcely knows how to stand upright'.[3] The philosopher had long ago identified his own everyday lack of resolve, and nearly a decade of stress and ill health saw him usually willing to take the path of least resistance if it allowed him to preserve his usual calm. Despite all this, there is nothing other than Place's bad feeling to suggest a conspiracy. Given how poorly the business was run from the start, the fairest explanation is simply that Godwin had no concept of how deeply in debt he was. Indeed, he wrote to Clairmont while she was in Margate in May 1811 to confess that he had entirely forgotten a bill for £140 that he owed to Place himself.[4] The family had spent so many years transferring, consolidating and postponing their debts, they may not have known everyone they owed money to. Further details in the Margate letter suggest that he was frequently surprised when he received demands for repayment. Place on several occasions angrily refused to give Godwin any more help with his finances, but through a combination of reasoned argument, excuses and pleading, the philosopher convinced Place to persist in his efforts until the businessman's patience was finally exhausted in late 1814.

Godwin's family was growing up, something that no doubt put increasing strain on their finances. Fanny, now almost an adult, was pressed into service at the shop. Godwin described her as quiet, sober and observing in her manner. He was sincerely attached to her, having refused an offer from Wollstonecraft's sisters to take her away and educate her at boarding school some years earlier. He noted his conversations with her as he did his adult friends. Later events imply that she felt the stress of running the Juvenile Library as acutely as he did. Godwin mostly educated his daughters at home, but sent his sons to school. This is more consistent than it seems: Godwin's daughters followed a curriculum similar to that of their brothers (languages, history, philosophy), an education that few girls' schools would have offered. Charles and William had been sent to Charterhouse, the London public school, though William would find it an unhappy place and eventually move to Charles Burney's school at Greenwich in 1814. In 1811, Charles left school to become an apprentice at Archibald Constable's publishing house in Edinburgh. Mary was also bound for Scotland. She had, for some years, experienced outbreaks of an unidentified skin condition on her right arm. The renowned surgeon Henry Cline was consulted, but no course of treatment proved particularly effective. The condition was probably aggravated by the fraught atmosphere of the house; Mary was placed for a time at a boarding school in Ramsgate, where she could bathe in the sea, but she did not seem to enjoy the experience and returned home in December 1811. Cline recommended more time by the sea and, in the summer of 1812, Godwin arranged for Mary to stay with the family of William Baxter (a well-wisher from the era of the 1794 Treason Trials) in Dundee. Many of the future novelist's biographers have inferred that the real reason for Mary's extended periods of convalescence was friction with Clairmont: Fanny Derham in Mary's 1835 novel *Lodore* spends her childhood away from home for that reason, and the novelist's letters as an adult betray a profound dislike of her stepmother. Given the effects of the family's strife on everyone else in the house however, this may only have been one element out of many.

The extended 'family' at Skinner Street included a succession of young men that sought Godwin's help and advice. The philosopher had always attracted such. It usually began with an unsolicited letter, or a call at the shop. John Arnot had arrived in this manner. Tom Turner had turned up on 4 July 1803 (having written the same day) and been a constant fixture for six years until Godwin had imposed strict ground rules for when Turner was allowed to visit. The philosopher always replied to the letters (though he sometimes took months to do so) and offered support where he could. A young man named Patrickson had been a promising pupil at Charterhouse but had become estranged from his family – Godwin solicited help from richer friends to send Patrickson to Cambridge University without his family's support, while simultaneously counselling the youth on how to repair his relationship with his mother.

When Godwin received a letter from another such young man at the beginning of January 1812, it came as no great surprise. The correspondent was an ardent admirer who had only recently learned that Godwin was still alive. The missive was passionate, but vague:

You will be surprised at hearing from a stranger. – No introduction has, nor in all probability ever will authorize that which common thinkers would call a liberty; it is however a liberty which altho' not sanctioned by custom is so far from being reprobated by reason, that the dearest interests of mankind imperiously demand that a certain etiquette of fashion should no longer keep 'man at a distance from man' and impose its flimsy fancies between the free communication of intellect. The name of Godwin has been used to excite in me feelings of reverence and admiration, I have been accustomed to consider him a luminary too dazzling for the darkness which surrounds him, and from the earliest period of my knowledge of his principles I have ardently desired to share on the footing of intimacy that intellect which I have delighted to contemplate in its emanations. ... My course has been short but eventful. I have seen much of human prejudice, suffered much from human persecution; yet I see no reason hence inferable which should alter my wishes for their renovation. The ill-treatment I have met with has more than ever impressed the truth of my principles on my judgement. I am young – I am ardent in the cause of philanthropy and truth, do not suppose that this is vanity. I am not conscious that it influences this portraiture. I imagine myself dispassionately describing the state of my mind. I am young – you have gone before me, I doubt not are a veteran to me in the years of persecution – is it strange that defying prejudice as I have done, I should outstep the limits of custom's prescription, and endeavor to make my desire useful by friendship with William Godwin?[5]

The letter writer was nineteen-year-old Percy Bysshe Shelley. Godwin wrote back swiftly, chiding Shelley for writing an introduction that told him little about its author. Shelley's reply arrived a few days later, explaining that he was 'the Son of a man of fortune in Sussex', heir to £6,000 a year, whose life had been changed by reading *Political Justice*. He had given up fantastic tales (he had written two gothic romances) in favour of atheism, and was writing 'an inquiry into the causes of the failure of the French revolution to benefit mankind'.[6] They exchanged more letters. Shelley explained his plan to take 'the benevolent and tolerant deductions of Philosophy' to Ireland to help those who Catholicism had kept ignorant. He had written a pamphlet, which he sent to Godwin (its size forced Godwin to pay the substantial excess postage). The philosopher, who had already written Shelley a letter of introduction to present to Curran, was concerned by what he read. *An Address, to the Irish People* condemned religious intolerance and declared that a religion was only as good as it helped people towards virtue and wisdom. It celebrated universal brotherhood and denounced violence. It exhorted the Irish to 'think, read and talk', to reform themselves (improve, in a Godwinian sense, but Shelley lays particular emphasis on resisting the vices the Irish were stereotypically accused of) in order to present a moral example that could not be denied the political rights that they were owed. Godwin wrote back to commend the pamphlet's sentiments, but to caution against its dissemination. The pamphlet proposed the establishment of a peaceful association for moral and intellectual improvement (his next pamphlet set down a programme for one). Godwin, still a critic of mass movements and political parties, told Shelley that such an organisation was intrinsically dangerous – even more so in the volatile context of Irish politics.

> … associations, organized societies, I firmly condemn, you may as well tell the adder not to sting
>> You may as well use question with the wolf
>> You may as well for bid the mountain pines
>> To wag their high tops, and to make no noise,
>> When they are fretted with the gusts of heaven,

as tell organized societies of men, associated to obtain their rights, and to extinguish oppression, prompted by a deep aversion to inequality, luxury, enormous taxes and the evils of war, to be innocent, to employ no violence, and calmly to await the progress of truth.[7]

Shelley replied that Godwin had given him much to think about, but the poet continued down the same path, attending political meetings and proudly sending a newspaper cutting to his mentor where he (Shelley) had been mentioned. The philosopher grew increasingly alarmed, remonstrating with Shelley to 'save yourself and the Irish people from the calamities with which I see your mode of proceeding to be fraught'.[8] Godwin's letters eventually made an impression, and Shelley wrote (on 18 March) to say he had withdrawn his publications and was leaving Dublin. He admitted his short-sightedness but refused to accept that his pamphlets had been dangerous. Godwin dryly observed that Shelley was only 'half a convert' to his argument, but said that time would do the rest.[9] They continued to correspond as Shelley and his wife Harriet visited Wales and Devon.

The episode contrasts sharply with the disingenuous, 'heartless' Godwin of Place's description. The early letters to Shelley show the philosopher instinctively falling into the role of teacher, willing to speak plainly and critically to a complete stranger, and in no way awed by his correspondent's claims of great wealth or literary talent. He also displays an obvious concern for Shelley's development and welfare, something he expresses in advice that reflects both his trademark gradualism and his experience of notoriety:

… it is highly improving for a man who is ever to write for the public, that he should write much while he is young. It improves him equally in the art of thinking, and of expressing his thoughts. Till we come to try to put our own thoughts upon paper, we can have no notion how broke and imperfect they are, or find where the imperfection lies. … But I see no necessary connection between writing and publishing, and least of all with one's name. The life of a thinking man who does this, will be made up of a series of Retractions. It is beautiful to correct our errors, to make each day a comment on the last, and to grow perpetually wiser; but all this need not be done before the public. … Mankind will ascribe little weight and authority to a versatile character, that makes a show of his imperfections. How shall I rely upon a man, they cry, who is not himself in his public character at all times the same? I have myself, with all my caution, felt some of the effects of this.[10]

Godwin had argued since the 1790s that a willingness to change one's mind was a sign of intellectual rigour but here he again acknowledges how easily transparency can be (wilfully) misconstrued, to the detriment of what the individual is trying to say. As in his letter to Louisa Holcroft, Godwin endorses accuracy (or here, clarity) over the duty to tell all the truth we know. The philosopher is happy to allow that his correspondent may one day have some great insight to convey to the community, but reflection and maturity will make it a better insight. The communication of truth ultimately requires patience. Godwin almost certainly did not see this as a retraction of his own – he never revises his belief in sincerity as an absolute duty – but it does represent a pragmatic compromise with the real world. He would come to make many more in his relationship with Percy Shelley.

Shelley encouraged Godwin to visit him in Lynmouth, on the Devon coast. For some months, Godwin declined the invitations, but finally at the end of August he seems to have written to signal his acceptance. He set out on 9 September. Events that week are unclear; the diary notes cryptically 'execution' on the 8th and records a flurry of calls to Place, Longdill (Shelley's lawyer, who Godwin knew socially) and others, followed by two calls on 'Bagley's banker' the following day before the philosopher caught a coach to Slough. Godwin's biographer William St Clair has advanced the theory that the diary refers to an order of execution and that one of the philosopher's many creditors had sent bailiffs to arrest him. While leaving London would certainly have kept Godwin out of debtor's prison (and perhaps allowed him to negotiate a bail-out from Shelley), we have little evidence to suggest anything so dramatic – Godwin probably gave Shelley advance notice of his journey (the diary records 'write to Shelley' on 31 August, and again on 7 September, but the letters themselves are no longer extant) and Godwin's letters to Clairmont while he was on the road make no mention of any difficulties at home. The journey was long and, at the age of 56, quite arduous – coach travel was notoriously uncomfortable, and the sea leg of Godwin's journey (from Bristol to Lynmouth) was interrupted by bad weather. The philosopher arrived in Lynmouth on the 18 September, having not eaten for two days. Shelley was not there, and had not been there for three weeks. Godwin experienced another attack of 'deliquium' that night, his second in as many days. He arrived back in London on the evening of the 25th, suffering two further attacks on the road and spending part of the journey as an 'outside' coach passenger (either sitting on the roof or riding in the luggage basket) exposed to the elements. The Shelleys arrived in London on 4 October and dined with the Godwins the same day.

Shelley became Godwin's almost daily companion during his first fortnight in town. The philosopher recorded their topics of conversation: 'matter & spirit; atheism' on the 6th, 'utility & truth; party' on the 7th, 'clergy; church govt; germanism' on the 9th.[11] The two dined together frequently, sometimes with their wives and sometimes not. Godwin treated the younger man as his student, recommending things for him to read and shooting down what he considered to be Shelley's wilder political or philosophical ideas. On 31 October, Shelley presented his mentor with the manuscript of his first great philosophical poem, *Queen Mab*. The work's debt to Godwin is obvious – describing a series of dream visions that look forward to a future where humanity has outgrown tyranny through moral improvement, and lives at peace with itself and nature. The philosopher read through the piece that day, though he did not make notes until he read the published version a year later.

The Shelleys departed London suddenly in mid-November, heading back to Wales without telling Godwin of their plans. The philosopher took up his pen once more, and their correspondence resumed. 'You have what appears to me a false taste in poetry', Godwin wrote to Shelley on 10 December, 'You love a perpetual sparkle and glittering, such as are to be found in Darwin, and Southey, and Scott, and Campbell.' The philosopher advised the young poet to read Milton, and that poet would prove a significant influence on both men for some time to come.

In the new year, Godwin made another influential friend, the philanthropist (later, socialist) Robert Owen. The two met at a dinner held by the journalist, Daniel Stuart, at which Coleridge was also present. Godwin and Owen had much to talk about and soon Owen was a regular visitor and dinner guest at Skinner Street. Owen had little in common with the passionate young men that usually sought the philosopher's acquaintance, however. In his early forties when he first met Godwin, Owen was a successful industrialist and a follower of Jeremy Bentham, and he had his own ideas but an open mind. Owen was a pioneer of the industrial community – philanthropic endeavours to improve worker's conditions had steadily gained purchase over the eighteenth century, but Owen's textile mill at New Lanark was notable for its comprehensive support of worker's health, education, and economic independence. At the time working on the essays that would form the first edition of *A New View of Society* (1813), Owen allowed Godwin to steer him away from a Benthamite conception of self-interest and towards the idea of universal benevolence. Like Godwin, Owen held that people were shaped by the world around them and that poverty, ignorance, and exploitation prevented the majority of humanity from accessing the means of moral improvement. In contrast to Godwin, however, Owen argued that this placed a duty on institutions to provide those means; that it was the responsibility of those in power to enable the improvement of ordinary people. Recalling the strict routines of industrial production, Owen's vision is benevolently authoritarian and would go on to influence the creation of the modern welfare state. Despite their radically different conclusions, Owen considered Godwin to be one of his major philosophical inspirations.

Around this time, Godwin began work on another biography. It was his first full-length work for adults since finishing *Faulkener* nearly six years earlier. *The Lives of Edward and John Phillips, Nephews and Pupils of Milton* (1815) took nearly two years to complete. Conceptually, the work is fascinating: Godwin's book is, in part, a look at Milton from the outside – an exploration of how and why the poet's pupils came to reject him as a religious teacher (both became critics of Puritanism) but not as a literary one (both were accomplished poets and literary critics). Based on contemporary accounts, including one by Edward himself, Godwin imagines Milton as a passionate and powerful educator. The brothers rejected his way of life, Godwin argues, in part because it is in the nature of pupils to rebel – to seek out truth for oneself rather than simply to receive it. Once out on their own, the brothers found worldly temptations too strong to go back to the Puritan life (the philosopher cannot help but criticise this as in some degree venal). Yet the brothers found happiness (and success) as poets because their education had awakened their potential.

Shelley returned to London in April, but made no attempt to see Godwin. The two ran into one another on 8 June. Harriet and Percy's first child, Elizabeth Ianthe Shelley, was born later that month. On 4 August, Shelley turned twenty-one. Now legally an adult, he could enter into contracts without parental consent. Shelley's enthusiasm had led him to commit to at least one expensive project already: a land-improvement scheme where he had stayed in Wales. At the end of 1812, Place had told Godwin that his only hope to avoid bankruptcy and prison was to convince Shelley to provide him with a substantial sum of money. What conversations Godwin and Shelley had over the subject are not recorded, but the poet had frequently written of his desire to use his fortune to support the less fortunate and (according to Place) Godwin was often very persuasive. Regardless of whatever offers of support the poet might have made, for a long time Shelley did nothing to actually raise whatever money Godwin might have asked for. Shelley's father had already granted him an allowance of £200 a year (a comparable income to a middle-class family of the period) but the poet would need to organise other means if he wished to raise significant amounts of capital. Shelley's family did not approve of his political agitation, or his marriage, and restricted his access to their wealth in hopes of bringing him under control.[12] The principal method of raising money open to the poet was the selling of post-obituary bonds, essentially obtaining a cash loan to be repaid (with considerable interest) when the recipient came into their inheritance. This was a high-stakes business, as the creditors were speculating on both the debtor surviving long enough to inherit and the value of the estate when they did so. Shelley was a good prospect: his grandfather (the current baronet) was eighty-two and his father nearly sixty, but his constant travelling and willingness to publish his work at his own expense (he arranged a private printing of *Queen Mab* that year) meant that he was racking up significant debts. The couple came and went from London continually in that year, allegedly to stay ahead of creditors. On 10 December, Shelley turned up for breakfast at Skinner Street without warning, was a near-constant presence for nearly a week, and then left London for Windsor.

At the suggestion of either Place or John King, Godwin convinced Shelley to auction a post-obit in order to raise money for the Juvenile Library. The auction took place on 3 March 1814, with an £8,000 bond offered to the highest bidder. Godwin's target was again in the region of £3,000 – the diary notes the figure £3,860 around this time, without further context – but the auction only raised £2,593, and the purchasers raised questions about the security of their investment. The final balance was not paid over until 6 July. Worse for Godwin, Shelley decided to keep half the money for himself. His reasons for doing so presented a more immediate crisis for the family.

Mary had returned home from Dundee on 30 March. She and her sisters were entranced by the handsome, charismatic young man who had won their father's respect and seemed poised to deliver the family from its constant financial woes. For his own part, Shelley took particular interest in Mary – he had seen little of her in the two years he had known Godwin, meeting her almost for the first time when she was sixteen. To Shelley, she must have seemed to embody the best qualities of both her illustrious parents: her mother's passion and her father's mind (he had, perhaps, read the *Memoir*). He wrote a poem to her dark eyes and trembling lips. By mid-June, Shelley was at Skinner Street every day, taking Mary on walks to her mother's grave in St Pancras churchyard (usually with Jane as chaperone). On 26 June, Mary declared her love for him. Shelley went to Godwin, perhaps to ask for his blessing. The poet was a vehement critic of marriage, and had only been persuaded to marry Harriet through being made to see the punishment society handed out to 'fallen' women. He had grown apart from Harriet, he had met someone new. He looked into legally separating from his wife (he asked Basil Montagu to find out what could be done), but he hoped to live with Harriet as his friend and Mary as his lover. He seemed sure that Godwin would approve, recalling the philosopher's own critique of marriage in *Political Justice*. The philosopher did not.

Precisely what Godwin thought is unknown. In late middle age he had made his peace with the institution of marriage, allowing that it was possible for two mutually complementary individuals to be happy together, and that its evils were primarily problems of implementation (his old bugbear, the law) rather than principle. He was also acutely aware that the scandal of what Shelley was proposing would fall far harder on Mary and Harriet than it would Percy. Godwin's account of their discussion says that he 'expostulated with him with all the energy of which I was master and with so much effect that for the moment he promised to give up his licentious love, and return to virtue'.[13] The exact order of events is ambiguous. Shelley biographers have traditionally claimed that Percy took his news to Godwin the day after Mary declared her love (27 June) and that the philosopher demanded that Shelley stay away from Skinner Street. Godwin's version of events places the revelation on the day the bond was paid (6 July) and the implication is that Shelley took his own share of the money to support both Harriet and Mary. The diary records that Shelley remained a regular visitor to Skinner Street between the 27 June and 6 July, but that all but one of Godwin's meetings with Shelley after the 6th took place away from the house (the one exception is where Harriet is also present). Godwin tried in vain to bring Percy and Harriet closer together – Percy insisted that his affection for Harriet was that of a brother; Harriet revealed that she was again pregnant. Mary was confined to the house. Shelley's later letters imply they either met or corresponded in secret. According to Clairmont, at one point Shelley stormed the shop and pressed a bottle of laudanum on Mary in the hope that she would join him in suicide. Clairmont's story presents Mary as one of the more level-headed members of the family: while Jane shrieked upon Shelley producing a pistol, Mary entreated the poet to calm himself and go home, promising her fidelity on condition that he reasonable.[14]

In the small hours of 28 July, Mary and Jane crept out of the house to meet Shelley waiting with a carriage. The trio escaped to Dover, booked space on a small boat heading to France that night and were blown by strong winds into Calais just before dawn. Clairmont gave chase and caught up with them on the evening of the 29th. Shelley prevented her from seeing Mary, but allowed her to talk to Jane. Clairmont successfully convinced her daughter to come home, but in the morning Shelley persuaded Jane that she should stay and Clairmont returned home in defeat. Godwin recorded the elopement in his diary the way he recorded a death in the family, simply by noting the time.

For a few weeks, it must have seemed as if one horror followed another. Patrickson dined with them on 8 August. Cambridge was a soul-destroying place for an outsider – without a gentleman's income, the young man was ostracised and abused. Godwin had done his best to support his friend, discussing the Stoics and sending money when he could. Patrickson returned to Cambridge the next day, wrote a letter to Godwin telling of his despair, and shot himself on 10 August. The same day, Godwin's son William ran away from home, almost certainly fleeing the atmosphere of the house, and was missing for two nights. On the business side of things, a deal to sell half the business for (another) £3,000 stalled over the value of the Juvenile Library's copyrights. Godwin was forced to write to Place to beg an extension on a loan of £300. Ironically, the family was experiencing cash-flow problems thanks to money owed them (they had received only a third of the money due for a substantial order of schoolbooks), but for Place it was the last straw. The businessman wrote an angry letter that condemned the philosopher's 'most selfish' conduct and claimed that he regretted ever trying to help him.[15] Godwin accused Place of trying to heap further miseries on him, after the events of the past few weeks, but over the course of their letters his tone became more indignant. Place accused him of insincerity, Godwin sent a high-handed reply that Place did not respond to. They did not see each other again socially for nearly two years, and Charles Clairmont (who returned home from Edinburgh in late 1814) was employed as a go-between. The sale of the business finally fell through at the end of September.

Shelley, Mary and Jane returned to England on 13 September. Their adventures had taken them through a France shattered by Russian, Prussian and Austrian armies (peace between the allies and France had only been declared in April), down into picturesque Switzerland, and returning back up the Rhine through Germany and the Netherlands. Mary was now pregnant. Godwin refused to speak to the trio, Shelley sent a letter on 16 September (Godwin notes it in his diary) but received no reply. The rest of the family attempted to make contact: Clairmont and Fanny ventured out to where the party were staying, but refused to speak to Shelley. Charles later approached under cover of darkness and stayed until three in the morning updating Shelley and his sisters on what had happened in their absence. Godwin finally wrote to Shelley on 22 September, stating 'with bitter invective', according to Shelley, that he wanted no more communication with them.[16] The situation dragged on for months, as friends and family attempted in vain to heal the breach. Shelley, like Godwin, was now being hounded by creditors. The poet lay low, keeping lodgings away from Mary and Jane (who was experimenting with new given names around this time, eventually settling on 'Claire'), but writing to Mary almost daily to arrange meetings. Mary's replies blame Clairmont for their estrangement:

> I detest Mrs. G she plagues my father out of his life & then – well no matter – Why will not Godwin follow the obvious bent of his affections & be reconciled to us – no his prejudices the world and *she* – do you not hate her my love – all these forbid it – What am I to do trust to time of course – for what else can I do?[17]

Mary underestimated the extent to which Godwin felt his children (and student) had betrayed him. As he explained to his backer, John Taylor, in a letter of 27 August, he had reposed 'the utmost confidence' in Shelley, but the poet had played 'traitor'. He had attempted to rouse, 'a sense of honor and natural affection in the mind of Mary', and believed that he had succeeded. 'They both deceived me'. He went on to say, however:

> I felt it however still to be my duty, not to desert myself, or so much of my family as was yet left to me, and even to provide, if possible for the hour of distress (which, I believe, is not far distant) when these unworthy children shall seek the protection and aid of their father.[18]

As in his angry dialogues with Mackintosh, Parr, and Place, when hurt, the philosopher fell back on stiff-necked pride as a defence. Godwin was perhaps waiting for his children to return chastened and penitent, but this did not diminish his sense of duty towards them, nor perhaps his love.

Whatever the reasons behind his long silence, Godwin was still willing to accept Shelley's money. In early November, Godwin failed to repay money he owed Lambert and called in a book auctioneer to help liquidate his stock. With Charles Clairmont still keeping him informed of events, Shelley stepped in to offer Lambert another post-obit and save the business. The poet exposed himself to considerable risk in helping – alerting London's financiers as to his whereabouts might easily have led to his arrest, and selling further post-obits essentially mortgaged his future in exchange for dwindling returns. Nevertheless, further bonds were offered to Place and other creditors. It is usually suggested that Godwin took Shelley's aid as no more than his due, certainly the bailout was consistent with the principles of utility and benevolence that both men held (the Juvenile Library was a project that contributed to general happiness, and Shelley had the means to help in its hour of need). Equally, it could be argued that many of Godwin's (current) financial problems were a direct result of Shelley's sudden change of heart regarding the earlier post-obit, thus the poet had a responsibility to fix the mess he had created. Yet the simplest explanation is that Godwin had little choice in the matter: the philosopher could choose to accept Shelley's help, or be declared bankrupt and probably sent to gaol.

On 30 November, Harriet gave birth to a son. She named the boy Charles. Shelley had tried repeatedly to persuade Harriet to come and live with Mary, Claire and himself as a family. His wife refused. He offered instead to support her financially, but at the time realistically lacked the money to do so. Harriet told a friend that Godwin had corrupted Shelley, and Mary believed that Harriet was involved in spreading rumours about her father.[19] In the new year, Shelley's grandfather died and the poet negotiated with his father (the new baronet) for money to clear some of his debts and to increase his income. This was at least partially successful, though the legal wrangling took a considerable amount of time. Shelley's father provided his son with an annuity of £1,000 a year and a one-off payment of over £4,000, granting him considerable financial independence. The poet settled £200 a year on Harriet and authorised a £300 banker's draft for Mary. On 22 February, Mary gave birth to a girl. The baby was premature and died in less than two weeks. The child's death haunted her – she suffered nightmares for years afterwards – but she was soon pregnant again.

Godwin's *Lives of Edward and John Phillips* was published in May 1815, in a print run of only 250 copies, of which fewer than 200 sold. The book received a handful of positive reviews, however, including one from Mackintosh. Two weeks later he had picked up his pen once more to protest the Declaration of the Congress of Vienna (to which Britain was a signatory) outlawing Napoleon for his return from exile. Godwin argued that the allied nations had no right to intervene in the internal affairs of France – if the French people chose Bonaparte over the Bourbons, they could do so. Napoleon had demonstrated his willingness to accept constitutional government and offered peace with the rest of Europe, while the allied governments had already violated the treaty that had exiled the Emperor a year earlier. Boldly, Godwin declared that he was 'too much the friend of man, and too little the citizen of a particular country' to wish Britain victorious. His letter was published in the *Morning Chronicle* on the 25th, but the philosopher continued to write and authored a second letter, packaging the two together for publication in a pamphlet. The work was printed on 22 June, the same day that Napoleon abdicated for the second time. Godwin withdrew the pamphlet. The moment had passed.

The Juvenile Library still lurched from one crisis to another. Finally, desperately, he wrote to Shelley directly on 11 November. The poet wrote back immediately, and the two conducted a terse correspondence on finances for several months. On 24 January 1816, Mary gave birth to her second child – a boy this time – which she named William, after her father. Shelley told Godwin that he intended to take his new family to Italy, sending the philosopher into a state of agitation. Godwin summoned Tom Turner (who Shelley did not like) to advise him. The letters thawed a little, but Godwin continued to pester Shelley for money while refusing to see him face to face. Eventually Shelley snapped:

> My astonishment, and I will confess when I have been treated with most harshness and cruelty by you, my indignation has been extreme, that, knowing as you do my nature, any considerations should have prevailed on you to have been thus harsh and cruel. I lamented also over my ruined hopes, of all that your genius once taught me to expect from your virtue, when I found that for yourself, your family, and your creditors, you would submit to that communication with me which you once rejected and abhorred, and which no pity for my poverty or sufferings, assumed willingly for you, could avail to extort. Do not talk of *forgiveness* again to me, for my blood boils in my veins, and my gall rises against all that bears the human form, when I think of what I, their benefactor and ardent lover, have endured of enmity and contempt from you and from all mankind.[20]

Godwin's response was not conciliatory, but neither did he bite back. The next day he wrote plainly, 'If I understand you, you will accept no kindness without approbations; and torture cannot wring from me an approbation of the act that separated us'. Shelley softened his tone. Using money from Shelley, Godwin published new editions of *Caleb Williams* and *St Leon* in the hope of generating quick profits.

In April, the philosopher travelled to Edinburgh to meet with Charles's old employer, the publisher Archibald Constable, and was able to negotiate a contract for a new novel. Constable introduced him to the city's intellectual elite: Francis Jeffrey, editor of the *Edinburgh Review*; Dugald Stewart, then Scotland's most prominent philosopher; and Walter Scott, then known principally as a poet, but already on his way to becoming the most successful novelist of the nineteenth century. All three were Godwin's ideological opponents, Tory writers who had joined in the abuse of the philosopher and his work decades earlier, but Godwin appears to have enjoyed their company regardless.[21] His journey back took him through the Lake District, where he spent an awkward day or two with Wordsworth (both were great friends of Coleridge, but neither was keen on the other). When he arrived back in London, he found that Shelley had delivered on his plan to leave the country. He left a letter and instructions to provide Godwin with more money:

> I respect you, I think well of you, better perhaps than of any other person whom England contains, you were the philosopher who first awakened, & who still as a philosopher to a very great degree regulate my understanding. It is unfortunate for me that the part of your character which is least excellent should have been met by my convictions of what was right to do. But I have been too indignant, I have been unjust to you. – forgive me. – burn those letters which contain the records of my violence, & believe that however what you erroneously call fame & honour separate us, I shall always feel towards you as the most affectionate of friends.[22]

Godwin set to work on his new novel (eventually titled *Mandeville*) with enthusiasm, but events soon took a darker turn. Sheridan died on 7 July. It was the end of an era in both politics and the theatre. Godwin noted his visits to the playwright's grave. He struggled to sleep at night. Shelley, Mary and Claire returned to Britain in September. They had met Byron in Switzerland and now Claire was pregnant with his child. They spent a few days in London (Godwin still refused to see them, and Claire's letters imply she was keen for her pregnancy to remain a secret) but the trio set up residence in Bath. Godwin began writing letters about money again, desperately in need of £300. Shelley's reply was sympathetic but offered little:

> I am exceedingly sorry to dissappoint you again. I cannot send you £300 because I have not £300 to send. I enclose within a few pounds the wrecks of my late negotiation with my father.
>
> In truth, I see no hope of my attaining speedily to such a situation of affairs as should enable me to discharge my engagements towards you. My fathers main design, in all the transactions which I have had with him, has gone to tie me up from all such irregular applications

of my fortune. In this he might have failed had he not been seconded by Longdill, & between them both I have been encompassed with such toils as were impossible to be evaded. When I look back I do not see what else I could have done than submit: what is called firmness would have, I sincerely believe left me in total poverty.[23]

Fanny wrote to Mary the next day describing their father's reaction: 'Shelley's letter came like a thunderclap. I watched Papa's countenance while he read it (not knowing the contents), and I perceived that Shelley had written in his most desponding manner.'[24] The sum that Shelley offered fell short of what the family needed and, against Godwin's instructions, the cheque was made out in his name (Godwin insisted that his name be kept off any promissory notes that Shelley sent him, perhaps to keep a low profile from creditors). Fanny suddenly left home on 7 October, taking a coach due west. She wrote to Godwin and Mary separately the next day; both letters were alarming enough that, when they arrived on the 9th, both Godwin and Shelley immediately took to the road in search of Fanny. Godwin returned home at two in the morning without further information. On the evening of the 9th, in a small room above the Mackworth Arms, Swansea, Fanny committed suicide with laudanum. Her last note read:

I have long determined that the best thing I could do was to put an end to the existence of a being whose birth was unfortunate, and whose life has only been a series of pain to those persons who have hurt their health in endeavouring to promote her welfare. Perhaps to hear of my death will give you pain, but you will soon have the blessing of forgetting that such a creature ever existed as[25]

The last part of the page was torn off, where there might have been a signature. The only identification she had were the initials M.W. on her stays (her mother's) and a G. on her stockings. Shelley arrived in Swansea on 11 October; Godwin had reached Bath but did not attempt to meet his daughters. He wrote to both Mary and Shelley about the need to keep the matter quiet, forbidding Shelley from claiming the body. The poet agreed, and Fanny was buried anonymously. Arriving home in London, Godwin wrote to Shelley:

I did indeed expect it.

I cannot but thank you for your strong expressions of sympathy. I do not see, however, that that sympathy can be of any service to me; but it is best. My advice and earnest prayer is that you would avoid anything that leads to publicity. Go not to Swansea; disturb not the silent dead; do nothing to destroy the obscurity she so much desired that now rests upon the event. It was, as I said, her last wish ... I said that your sympathy could be of no service to me, but I retract the assertion; by observing what I have just recommended to you, it may be of infinite service.

Godwin went on to write that he and Clairmont had contemplated telling people that Fanny had gone to see her aunts in Ireland, and begged Shelley to allow them the right to use their own discretion in the matter. He thanked the poet for helping to keep the matter out of the newspapers. They had not at that point told anyone what had happened. Their son Charles, who had been travelling Europe since the spring, did not receive the news until he returned home in the summer of 1817.

On 10 December Harriet Shelley's body was recovered from the Serpentine. She had been missing for three weeks. Harriet had been pregnant, though it was not clear who the father was. Her family responded in much the same way the Godwins had, burying her under a false name. Shelley fought for custody of their children, but her family resisted. Harriet's last wish had been that her sister Eliza take care of Ianthe (Charles was not mentioned in her final letter), but the poet's de facto abandonment of his children – he had not seen Ianthe since 1814 – would have been enough for the Westbrook family to believe that Shelley was not a suitable guardian. Longdill advised the poet that marriage to Mary would end 'all pretences to detain the children' and (implicitly) grant him his full parental rights.[26]

Shelley wrote to Godwin informing him of Harriet's death and, on 18 December, called at Skinner Street to discuss matters with Clairmont. Godwin wrote to Mary on Christmas Eve, the first time he had done so since the elopement. On Boxing Day, Godwin wrote to Shelley, and the day after that Shelley called again. This time, Godwin received him. On the 28th, Godwin, Clairmont, Shelley and Mary met to discuss the situation. The only account of the conversation is Clairmont's: allegedly Shelley acknowledged his engagement to Mary but asked for the customary year of mourning for Harriet. On this he seemed intractable, until Mary put her hand on his shoulder and informed him that she would kill herself and their unborn child if he did not marry her promptly. Clairmont's story does not tally with the advice Shelley received from Longdill, but it provides a neatly ironic reversal of the suicide pact that she claimed the poet had proposed two years earlier. The truth of the meeting is probably more prosaic, but Clairmont's anecdote tells us something about her assessment of Shelley's character: as mercurial, prevaricating, and perhaps in need of a firm hand. Both Godwin's and Shelley's biographers have always regarded Mary Jane's version of events with some degree of scepticism – Clairmont was considered dishonest by many of Godwin's circle – but this, and the earlier suicide story, and her account of many other events, suggest someone compelled to turn events into a story (to tell 'tall tales' that suited her audience) rather than someone who misled others maliciously.[27]

Regardless of the negotiations, Mary and Percy were married on 30 December. Shelley described the wedding as 'magical in its effects', so effective was it in healing the breach between the two households:

> Mrs G and G were both present, and appeared to feel no little satis-
> faction. Indeed Godwin throughout has shown the most polished and
> cautious attentions to me and Mary. He seems to think no kindness
> too great in compensation for what has past. I confess I am not entirely
> deceived by this, though I cannot make my vanity wholly insensible
> to certain attentions paid in a manner studiously flattering. Mrs. G.
> presents herself to me in her real attributes of affectation, prejudice,
> and heartless pride.[28]

The estrangement was, to all extents and purposes, over. Godwin and Shelley would fight again in the future; Mary would at times keep her father at arm's length; but never again would Godwin sever contact with his daughter and son-in-law. Claire had her baby Alba (later renamed Allegra) in January 1817. The matter remained a secret, for some time the Shelleys maintained the fiction that Claire was looking after the child of a friend, and nothing indicates that the Godwins were aware of Alba's parentage until her christening in March. Shelley lost his custody battle the same month – the court decided against the poet on 17 March, the Westbrooks' case against him hinging on Shelley's politics as much as his actual neglect of his wife and children – but the matter was not fully settled until a year later, when Ianthe and Charles were placed in the care of a third party (a couple called the Humes), and Shelley was only granted visiting rights under supervision. The Shelleys and Claire settled in Marlow, outside London. They visited the Godwins, and Godwin came to stay with them in the spring. Mary's third child, Clara, was born in September. The birth only briefly interrupted Mary's literary endeavours: through August to October she compiled *A History of a Six Weeks Tour* (a collage of the trio's travels in 1814), while Shelley attempted to negotiate her a publisher for her first novel – *Frankenstein*.

John Philpott Curran died in October. Godwin dedicated the soon-to-be-finished *Mandeville* to his friend's memory. The philosopher's dwindling circle of literary and political veterans began to overlap with Shelley's network of new talents. Hazlitt argued politics all night with Shelley and the poet's confidant, Leigh Hunt. In November, Godwin was introduced to a young John Keats when the latter called on Shelley during dinner (Keats's friend, Charles Dilke, was an ardent admirer of *Political Justice*; Keats himself had been greatly influenced by reading 'Edward Baldwin's' *The Pantheon* as a boy). Around the same time, the philosopher acquired a new 'student' in the form of Henry Blanch Rosser. Rosser would go on to prove an able research assistant.

Mandeville was finally published in December 1817. The story is set during the period of the Commonwealth (the years between the execution of Charles I and the Restoration). It is a dark, savage, novel about a society coping with trauma. The world of Cromwell's Interregnum is a haunted one; every family has a father or brother or son that died a hero in the wars, and that hero casts a shadow over the next generation. The protagonist's social ties place him among the Protestant Royalists, a faction under constant pressure to prove its loyalty to the exiled king because of its unwillingness to embrace the more Catholic culture of his court. A series of humiliations encourage Charles Mandeville's already burgeoning misanthropy. The emergence of a rival, Clifford, who seems to be everything Charles is not, tests him further. As in all of Godwin's major fictional works, the novel recounts the protagonist's downward spiral in the first person. The narrative is self-consciously literary: the text makes extensive use of Biblical and literary quotation (primarily Milton's *Comus*) from period sources, Godwin making a number of historical allusions in the text that point towards a particular date of 'composition' (that is, when the protagonist supposedly authored the manuscript) and providing a sophisticated insight into the narrator's mental space. The protagonist's narration becomes stranger and more incoherent over the course of the novel, reaching a wild and gothic peak in the third volume, as his obsession with Clifford overcomes whatever good was left within him.

The novel is an indictment of the obsession with martyrdom that Godwin saw within Dissenting culture. Like the philosopher himself, the protagonist was raised on stories of men and women who died bravely (and usually gruesomely) for God. The protagonist searches for a death that will give meaning to his life – in direct contrast to Clifford, who celebrates life however he finds it. It is easy to infer a certain amount of morbidity on the part of the author too – the deaths of Sheridan and Curran while he was writing no doubt reminded Godwin of his own mortality, but this seems trivial next to the lonely end of both Fanny and Harriet. One of *Mandeville*'s principal themes is that of isolation; the suicides no doubt played on the philosopher's mind.

A few weeks later, on 1 January 1818, Mary published *Frankenstein* with Lackington and Co. It was a small print run, but the novel sold readily. The work went out anonymously (not unusual at the time), but a page before the preface dedicated the novel to Godwin, and reviewers quickly detected the philosopher's influence running through the text. It is clearly a first novel. The 1818 version of *Frankenstein* is spiky in places: readers often find it difficult to sympathise with the characters, its literary references are poetic but improbable, and its philosophical argument is highly ambiguous.[29] The debts to Godwin are obvious: *Frankenstein* is a tale of persecution and pursuit (like *Caleb Williams*), using alchemy as a plot device (like *St Leon*) and Switzerland as its rural idyll (*St Leon* again, *Fleetwood*), and leaning heavily on Milton for its poetic allusions (*Mandeville*). Many assumed that Shelley had written the novel – he had written the preface – but the manuscript, in Mary's hand with Percy's comments in the margin, displays editorial interventions rather than a guiding hand. Few literary works spring out of nothing, and listing *Frankenstein*'s influences does not detract from its striking originality. That the novel takes a fantastic idea and uses it to explore moral and political responsibility might reasonably place it in Godwin's literary 'school', but Mary's use of overlapping narrative frames (the creature tells his story to Frankenstein, who tells his story to Walton, who tells his story to us) show her developing rather than simply imitating those literary techniques. The story's lack of moral clarity – its principal characters are, at best, antiheroes – also illustrates Mary's independence from both her father and husband philosophically. In Godwin's novels, characters espouse moral principles that they fail to live up to; in *Frankenstein*, the principles themselves are open to question – high-mindedness is indistinguishable from ambition, domestic values carry the suggestion of incest, and it is the fate of a man and his creator to be locked into a cycle of reciprocal suffering. Whereas *Caleb Williams* ended with a victory for truth (however poignant), *Frankenstein* ends with mutual annihilation.

Godwin continued to ask Shelley for money. The poet had his own problems. Still hounded by his own creditors, Shelley was arrested for debt at the beginning of October 1817 (how the situation was resolved is unknown). Nevertheless, the poet replied to Godwin's requests with admirable patience. Perhaps Shelley understood the extent to which the philosopher's other sources of borrowing had dried up: Wedgwood, Johnson and Curran were all dead; Place was adamant in his refusal to spend money to help the Godwins (and not simply Godwin himself – Place had turned down a business proposal from Charles in 1815); Lambert and other creditors had gradually turned hostile in recent years. Shelley continued to funnel money to Godwin – he also raised money for Leigh Hunt – but his relationship with the philosopher gradually soured once more. The letters that survive from this period veer between sympathy, hostility, entitlement and distrust; but what is apparent in all of Godwin's letters about money is that the philosopher begs money to support others rather than himself. His letters to Place stress the difficulty of supporting a large family – Place dismissed this, implying that Godwin had been under no obligation to adopt other men's children – but the businessman had earlier observed that Godwin sometimes borrowed money in order to help people in greater need than himself, pushing himself deeper into debt so that he could repay loans owed to friends who urgently needed the money returned.[30] Godwin's borrowing was obviously financially unsound, but Place's comment suggests both a tendency to respond short-sightedly to crisis and a willingness to take great personal risks on behalf of others. At the end of 1817, it was Marshall who was in need. Godwin immediately organised a subscription to help him. While Shelley begged poverty, Godwin contributed £13 to the fund – an amount the philosopher almost certainly did not have to spare. It was Place who settled the majority of Marshall's debts, at Godwin's urging. When Place learned that the philosopher had also made a monetary contribution it reignited all of their old arguments, compounding the ill will he already felt towards Godwin.

In January, encouraged by Percy's poor health and a determination to present baby Allegra to her father, the Shelleys finally resolved on a permanent move to Italy. Shelley had himself insured against the possibility of dying before his father, a move that allowed him to sell another post-obit. How much this raised is not clear (estimates range from £2,000 to £4,500) but the sum liable is known to have been £9,000. Some of this money went to Godwin (again, how much is unknown), but their surviving letters make it apparent that Shelley kept most of the money for himself. Godwin was dismayed – the tone of their correspondence implies that the philosopher did not trust Shelley's reasons for holding on to the money he had borrowed, and proposed that the money be held in a joint account that required their mutual agreement to access. Ultimately, however, Godwin attempted to move past the dispute:

Now to the main point. I will never again discuss with you any question of this sort upon paper; but I do not desire the presence of any third person.

Since our last conversation at Marlow, I have reflected much on the subject. I am ashamed of the tone I have taken with you in all our late conversations. I have played the part of a supplicant, and deserted that of a philosopher. It was not thus I talked with you when I first knew you. I will talk so no more. I will talk principles; I will talk Political Justice; whether it makes for me or against me, no matter. I am fully capable of this. I desire not to dictate. I know that every man's conduct ought to be regulated by his own judgement, such as it may happen to be. But I hold it to be my duty once to state to you the principles which belong to the case. Having done that, it is my duty to forbear.[31]

Shelley did not reply. Godwin continued to write (the diary records writing letters to Shelley throughout February), but there is no evidence of any reply from the poet. The two did not see each other again until 6 March, when Godwin dropped in to visit Mary and stayed until Percy returned. Poet and philosopher were reconciled to some extent; Godwin's diary records Shelley's calls for several days after. Godwin does not seem to have attended the christening of his grandchildren on 9 March (ostensibly conducted to cement a formal record of the children's parentage, particularly relevant for Byron's daughter Allegra). The diary notes a call from Shelley with others, but not any event – Godwin recorded weddings and funerals with the name of the church, and we might expect to find that here if that were the case. It is not possible to tell whether this indicates some continuing distance between the two households, or if Godwin merely saw no need to attend. The Shelleys left Britain on 12 March. Writing from Dover that day, the poet authorised his banker to pay Godwin another £150.

Skinner Street was now mostly empty. Of the children, only William remained. William was intermittently at school – he had left the Burney school at the end of 1817, and flitted from business school in Essex to an apprenticeship under the architect Peter Nicholson the year after (he would later try his hand at engineering before settling into journalism in his early twenties). For a time, the Godwins hosted Clairmont's nephew Marc Valette (while he attended school in London) but the house and shop were no longer the intellectual hub they had been during Shelley's visits, or the early years of the Juvenile Library. On 23 June 1818 they received an eviction notice. Godwin's refusal to pay rent had finally prompted legal intervention, but the philosopher continued to ignore the issue, allegedly closing the door on callers representing the landlords. The tactic worked, and Godwin succeeded in dragging the matter out for several more years.

Little Clara died in Venice in September. The family had travelled around northern Italy at breakneck pace, the heat and the disruption taxing the health of the whole party. Claire became ill, as did Shelley (though he was convinced he had been poisoned), but Clara was dangerously sick for weeks. The various illnesses may have been unrelated to each other, but Mary blamed the fatigue of travel for the dysentery and fever that eventually claimed the child's life. Godwin wrote to offer comfort, but his condolences were typically stoic:

> I sincerely sympathise with you in the affliction which forms the subject of your letter, and which I may consider as the first severe trial of your constancy and the firmness of your temper that has occurred to you in the course of your life. You should, however, recollect that it

is only persons of a very ordinary sort, and of a pusillanimous disposition, that sink long under a calamity of this nature.[32]

Godwin liked to imagine himself a purely rational creature. He knew that he was not, but distress often prompted him to retreat into a protective stoicism – he read Seneca when he was ill – that allowed him to pretend that physical and emotional demands were merely a storm to be weathered by those with greater things to address. It should come as no surprise that he recommended the same outlook to his daughter, though his autobiographical notes make it obvious that such fortitude was more aspiration than reality. William Shelley, still only three years old, died in Rome in June 1819, possibly a victim of the malaria epidemic that swept the city that summer. Mary fell into a period of serious depression. Shelley, perhaps struggling with grief himself but certainly at a loss as to how to help his wife, asked Godwin to write to Mary. The news struck the philosopher hard too, the diary noting 'depression' the day after he received Shelley's letter. Yet Godwin did not understand the depth of his daughter's unhappiness: she had lost three children and was pregnant with a fourth; Byron had taken his daughter Allegra and refused Claire access; rumours regarding Claire's intimacy with Shelley still plagued them. The philosopher, coming from a family where at least four of the children had died in infancy, tried tough love:

... allow me the privilege of a father, and a philosopher, in expostulating with you on this depression. I cannot but consider it as lowering your character in a memorable degree, and putting you quite among the commonality and mob of your sex, when I thought I saw in you symptoms entitling you to be ranked among those noble spirits that do honour to our nature.[33]

Chiding her to remember that she had 'all the goods of fortune' and great potential of her own, Godwin argued forcefully that his daughter not give up on life simply because she had lost an infant child. The philosopher's tone was strict but not, as Shelley later wrote, hard-hearted (a hard-hearted father would not have written at all). Exactly how Mary received her father's admonition is unclear, but a letter to her friend Amelia Curran shows that she derived no consolation from it. Shelley himself was appalled at Godwin's letters, not least because they included side-swipes at the poet's failings (the philosopher was again in desperate need of money he believed Shelley had promised to pay) and, after their next child was born (Percy Florence, on 12 November 1819), he took to withholding Godwin's letters from Mary to preserve her peace of mind.[34]

Mary's feelings of being torn between father and husband seem to find their expression in her novel *Mathilda*, begun a few months after William's death. The novel reverses the dynamics of Mary's own relationships: the poet Woodville is the heroine's platonic friend and listener, her father the wild and impassioned suitor – a man who confesses to an incestuous love for his daughter because he cannot bear to lose the last image of her departed mother to another man. We should naturally be wary of reading too much biographical insight into *Mathilda*, though all of the author's novels draw on elements of her own life. Mary sent the manuscript to Godwin to arrange its publication, but the philosopher was so shocked by the work that he refused to pass the manuscript on, or return it. The reactionary press had circulated rumours for years that Mary, Claire and Percy's relationship was somehow incestuous; Shelley himself had needed to be discouraged from placing an incestuous (brother–sister) relationship at the centre of the poem *Laon and Cythna* (later retitled *The Revolt of Islam*). Godwin wrote that he found much to admire in *Mathilda*, but regarded the incest as 'detestable'. While it would be fair to criticise the philosopher's decision to suppress his daughter's most challenging novel (it remained unpublished until the late twentieth century), we might also sympathise with Godwin's refusal to give their enemies the ammunition for a fresh round of assaults. Whether the philosopher acted out of cowardice or protectiveness is a matter of perspective, but the decision illustrates the man that Godwin had become.

The contrast between Godwin's pragmatism in 1820 and the principled stand of the 1790s encourages us to see a philosopher who had been beaten down by the consequences of his earlier bravery and who was quietly abandoning his principles to stay afloat. A key difference between the 1790s and the 1810s, however, is the addition of a large family and business to Godwin's concerns. What so much of Godwin's relationship with Percy and Mary Shelley demonstrates is the philosopher's willingness to compromise in order to protect the people around him. Godwin, as an individual, had lived the principles he espoused to the best of his ability (he outlined his own failings in writing on more than one occasion, and those shortcomings connect neatly with things he was criticised for throughout his life). As a father, husband and employer, he accepted a responsibility to accommodate 'things as they are' while still clinging on to the ideas that had made him hero or villain to the reading public.

8

The Pensioner
1819–36

In an 1819 letter to Lady Caroline Lamb, Godwin declared himself retired from practical politics. Seeking the philosopher's endorsement for her brother-in-law's parliamentary campaign, Lady Caroline wrote Godwin a courtly letter that betrayed the assumption that his apparent disengagement was a matter of principle:

> My dear madam, – You have mistaken me. Mr G. Lamb has my sincere good wishes. My creed is a short one. I am in principle a Republican, but in practice a Whig.
>
> But I am a philosopher: that is, a person desirous to become wise, and I aim at that object by reading, by writing, and a little by conversation. But I do not mix in the business of the world, and I am too old to alter my course, even at the flattering invitation of Lady Caroline Lamb.[1]

A few months later, mounted troops killed over a dozen people at St Peter's Fields in Manchester as they attempted to arrest the leaders of a mass meeting in support of parliamentary reform. The event quickly became known as the Peterloo Massacre, and provoked horror among reformers and radicals of every stripe (Godwin's diary records 'outrage at Manchester'). The atmosphere of the country became increasingly hostile. Outbreaks of anti-government violence occurred in Huddersfield and Burnley in the autumn, and the government responded with the Six Acts – a series of bills restricting the right of the people to assemble and extending taxes on publications to curtail printing by working-class radicals. In February 1820, revolutionaries attempted to assassinate the cabinet – the Cato Street Conspiracy – but were lured into a trap by government spies. Godwin noted many of these events but did not, as he had done in the 1790s or in 1815, reach for his pen to make public comment. He may have suffered a stroke in November 1818 (the diary merely notes 'paralysis') and in December 1819 seems to have lost the use of his left hand ('torpor'). His health had deteriorated steadily for over a decade; he recorded regular headaches and dizziness. Though always a believer in quiet reform over revolutionary action, the philosopher was finally too sick to join the (metaphorical) barricades.

Yet Godwin had always been more comfortable, and more confident, in the realm of theory. The philosopher may have considered himself 'retired' but he was still a man of interest for parliamentarians and radical thinkers, still sought after for his conversation on learned topics. Godwin still believed in the power of conversation to effect change – in late 1819 he wrote to and called on James Scarlett, the barrister tasked with prosecuting the Peterloo demonstrators. The details of what they might have discussed are lost, but Godwin might have been trying to steer Scarlett to a position similar to the one the philosopher expressed in the 1795 *Considerations*: critical of mass demonstration but emphatically rejecting government repression.[2] His exchange of letters with Lady Caroline Lamb began some years of friendship between them; Godwin spent a few days as the family's guest in 1822. Lady Caroline's husband, the future Lord Melbourne, would eventually serve as prime minister (and close confidant) to Queen Victoria. At the other end of the spectrum, the philosopher had in recent years become a friend of the satirist William Hone – a man whose deliberate provocation of the establishment had seen him tried for blasphemy, and acquitted, in what is now seen as a landmark case for British freedom of speech. Godwin felt that he had one last philosophical contribution to make: the comprehensive reply to Malthus that friends had urged him to write for nearly two decades. As he wrote to Clairmont, on one of her trips to Southend:

What matters what becomes of this miserable carcass, if I can live for ever in true usefulness? And this must be the case in the present instance: for whatever becomes of my individual book if I am right the system of Malthus can never rise again, and the world is delivered for ever from this accursed apology in favour of vice and misery, of hard-heartedness and oppression.[3]

His old rival had not been idle in that time, and now enjoyed a position as professor at the East India Company's training college at Haileybury. Malthus had continued to revise and expand the *Essay* every few years (1817 saw the publication of the fifth edition), and the mathematician's language had hardened. The collegial discussion of the original essay had gradually given way to a tone of authority, the debate with Godwin was pushed into the background, and the *Essay* read more and more like a justification of the status quo – in general, advocating the elimination of all forms of welfare support outside private charity (Malthus quotes the biblical 'he who does not work, neither shall he eat', with approval). Most appallingly for Godwin, Malthus consciously did not exempt children or the disabled from his rhetoric, arguing that communities had no moral obligation to care for abandoned children (indeed, that doing so only added to the underclass of the future) and proposing legal penalties for children born out of wedlock.

With the help of his disciple, Rosser, Godwin spent two years research-ing and writing his answer, publishing *Of Population* in November 1820. Time had given Godwin the space to question Malthus's breezy formula. No longer accepting an inevitable disparity between population growth and food production, Godwin now sought to prove that society's inequality was not a natural consequence of overpopulation. For all the mathematician dressed his theory up as a law of nature, it rested on patchy data. Now armed with two surveys worth of British census figures (1801 and 1811) and writing to obtain comparable information from the United States, Godwin was willing to argue that Britain was not, in fact, overpopulated – its inequality was the direct result of political and moral errors that Malthus's theory apparently sought to absolve. Since the *Reply to Parr*, Godwin and Malthus's relationship had cooled. It had been some years since the two had exchanged even coldly polite letters, and the book betrays a certain anger at seeing Malthus's theory lauded for essentially telling the political and economic establishment what it wanted to hear. Though Godwin's argument carries considerable moral force, two-thirds of the book is given over to the philosopher's own demographic research. *Of Population* uses census data from Sweden and Paraguay to provide examples of places where good living conditions have occurred alongside negligible population growth, while using information gathered from sources in Massachusetts to argue that the doubling of population

Malthus observed in the US was the result of immigration rather than an unrestricted birth rate.

Godwin's argument can be described as counter-reactionary: the most recent editions of Malthus's *Essay* endorsed 'things as they are', allowing Godwin to emphasise its distance from more traditional moral values. Throughout the book Godwin co-opts conservative rhetoric, describing the *Essay* as unchristian and reminding readers that, for all it served to rationalise away criticism of contemporary society, it was a work of philosophical 'innovation' that true conservatives should regard with suspicion. The philosopher's argument is not entirely successful – his appeals to religious values are hollow, though they do expose the hypocrisy of those among Malthus's defenders who were keen to denounce heterodoxy when it did not benefit them. Godwin is on stronger ground when he returns to progressive arguments; Malthus's *Essay* validates passivity and intellectual cowardice, asserting that attempts to improve humanity's lot are (at best) futile or (at worst) counterproductive. What Godwin attempts to show is that such a conclusion flies in the face of everything we know about ourselves as a culture. Historical data suggests that we adapt ourselves (and our communities) to the environment and the available resources, advancements in knowledge suggest that we can rise to the challenge of providing for larger populations in the future. Underlying Godwin's argument is the position that inequality is not a symptom of human misery, but its principal cause.

Of Population did not strike the death blow that Godwin apparently hoped it would. Malthus's existing critics welcomed the addition of figures that offered a different picture to those found in the *Essay*, and commended Godwin's challenge to the *Essay*'s principle argument regarding the United States. Malthus's supporters condemned the tone of Godwin's book, implied jealousy, and accused the philosopher of making personal attacks on his opponent. The reasonable criticism was made that Godwin's Swedish data was open to interpretation, but there was little common ground that would have allowed a more productive discussion. One influential reader who remained unconvinced was US President James Madison, who was forwarded a copy of Godwin's book by ambassador Richard Rush. Madison denounced Godwin's argument on US immigration as a slight on American fertility, though the President held his own complex opinions on the subject of population that ran contrary to those of Malthus.[4] The most abusive response came from

Malthus himself, however. Offered the chance to review the book (anonymously) in the *Edinburgh Review*, Malthus denounced *Of Population* as 'the poorest and most old-womanish performance that has fallen from the pen of any writer of name, since we first commenced our critical career'. The mathematician used his platform to accuse Godwin of misrepresentation, and asserted that the philosopher's research only served to make his own thesis incontrovertible.[5] Godwin had never been impressed with authors who wrote from the cover of anonymity to praise their own work (he had briefly fallen out with Coleridge on the subject, fifteen years earlier) and, on learning of the review, he complained of the abuse in a letter to Mary. He did not see Malthus again until 12 December 1822, a meeting the diary records as 'silent'.

Poverty and misery became very real considerations for the Godwins when they were finally evicted from Skinner Street in May 1822. After a series of legal battles, spanning several years, a man called Read was recognised as the lawful owner of the property. Court rulings also established Read's right to both evict his tenants and charge them for years of backdated rent. Shelley had refused the Godwins his assistance as far back as the summer of 1820, bitterly complaining of how little difference his money had ever made. Read sent bailiffs to prevent them from absconding with the Juvenile Library's stock. William Junior organised an immediate sale that allowed the family to salvage what was left of the business and reopen the shop at 195 Strand at the beginning of July.

On 4 August, news reached London that Shelley had drowned while sailing on the Ligurian Sea. Godwin was hurt to have received the news second-hand (from an agent of Leigh Hunt), not realising that Mary had herself been close to death only a few weeks earlier after a miscarriage left her bleeding uncontrollably. As she recovered, Mary wrote to her father regularly (the letters have since been lost).

After months of negotiation, the courts ordered Godwin to pay just short of £400 in rent arrears. The ever-dependable Marshall stepped in to persuade the publisher John Murray to organise a private subscription fund to pay the philosopher's debt. The amount raised fell short of what was needed but the list of subscribers records a host of distinguished names from Godwin's career, both of friends and adversaries from the literary and political world. Basil Montagu and Anthony Carlisle contributed, as did Byron. Walter Scott sent £10, on the understanding that his gift would remain private. Charles Lamb and Tom Turner had already given money to help the Juvenile Library escape Skinner Street. Mackintosh helped the subscription fund go public with the aim of raising more money. Mary volunteered the proceeds from her latest novel, *Valperga*, which Godwin edited for her and was published in February 1823. The Edinburgh publisher John Anderson sent word of his interest in publishing a new edition of *The Enquirer*. Read took what money had been raised by subscription and agreed to receive the rest in instalments. For a brief period, it seemed as if the storm had passed. Godwin was busy at work writing another history (of the Civil War and the Commonwealth), and Mary was finally on her way home.

Mary arrived back in London on 25 August, her father and brother waiting for her on the wharf as she arrived. She described the new house to Leigh Hunt as 'dismal' but 'infinitely better than the Skinner St. one'.[6] The first of many stage adaptations of *Frankenstein* (Richard Brinsley Peake's *Presumption*) was playing at the English Opera House when she returned – Mary could expect no money from it, but Godwin cannily arranged for the novel to be reprinted in order to capitalise on the play's success.[7] The play was a hit, spawning a host of imitators and parodies, and cementing *Frankenstein*'s image in the popular consciousness (many elements familiar to modern audiences from James Whale's 1931 film originally derive from Peake's adaptation). Peake's script dispenses with much of the novel's complexity – the creature is mute, and so unable to speak in its own defence – and delivers an unambiguous warning against hubris, along with comic and musical interludes. Mary, Godwin and William Junior saw the play a few days after her return; Mary's letter to Leigh Hunt records her amusement.

The first volume of Godwin's *History of the Commonwealth* appeared in 1824. Originally contracted by Henry Colburn to write two volumes, the philosopher allowed his enthusiasm to get the better of him once again. The final work spanned four volumes, the last mostly a study of Cromwell as a statesman, that Colburn was forced to publish in stages (as each volume was finished) until 1828. Godwin's work is noteworthy for being one of the earliest histories of the Civil War era to favour the parliamentarian cause. For over a century, the standard text on the period had been Clarendon's *History of the Rebellion* – as a royalist insider, the author had been present at many of the defining moments of the struggle, but his bias was clear. The only work of similar authority on the parliament side were the memoirs of Bulstrode Whitelock, but that was an altogether less accessible and less comprehensive text, known only to serious scholars of the period. Godwin's history is a conscious attempt to reset the balance. The philosopher was openly critical of Charles I – previous histories, relying on Clarendon's assessment of the monarch's intentions and motivations had erred on the side of sympathy – but avoided partisanship by condemning the intolerance of the religious independents on the other side. Godwin presented Cromwell as a complex character: a spiritual man who wielded power ruthlessly, a man who had fought to curtail the power of monarchy who found himself taking dictatorial powers when he found parliament wanting. The philosopher's admiration for Cromwell is clear, but he does not shy away from denouncing the Lord Protector's sometimes arbitrary use of authority.

The *History* was well-received but, as a large and expensive work, was never destined to become a popular success. The Juvenile Library struggled on until the nationwide financial crash of 1825, as out-of-control speculation caused the collapse of many small or regional banks – leaving businesses that ran on credit (as much of publishing industry did) in dire straits. Bankruptcy came as a relief for Godwin. The years of begging, arguing and dodging were finally over, and the fall had come at a time when even the most respected publishers were in danger of collapse. The Edinburgh publishers Archibald Constable and James Ballantyne were both bankrupted, and Walter Scott was almost ruined as a result. The family – now just really Godwin and Clairmont – moved from the Strand to a house in Gower Place. William was now a reporter for the *Morning Chronicle*, Mary engaged in a drawn-out battle with her in-laws over her right to publish her husband's work and custody of Percy Florence. Charles and Claire spent most of these years in Europe (Charles mostly in Vienna; Claire working as a governess in Moscow, and later Dresden) but made the time to return home and share their experiences. Through Mary and William, Godwin was introduced to another generation of writers: the American novelist James Fenimore Cooper, novelist and future MP Edward Bulwer-Lytton, the adventurer (and friend of Shelley) Edward Trelawny. Frances Wright (the abolitionist and US social reformer) introduced herself, writing to Godwin about the community she had built in Tennessee before she called at Gower Place with Robert Dale Owen in tow. The philosopher was not always the centre of attention, however, Robert Dale later confessed that he had become smitten with Mary, and Mary herself joked at the suggestion of a romance between herself and Godwin's old friend Washington Irving.

Release from the stress of the Juvenile Library sparked a renaissance in Godwin's writing. Less than a week after he sent the final volume of the *History* to his publisher, he had begun work on a new novel. *Cloudesley*, published in March 1830, is a rambling story that meanders from political intrigue in Russia to personal intrigue in Greece on its way to another exploration of Godwin's favourite theme – education, or rather the relationship between mentor and student. The story was inspired by the then famous Annesley case, where it was alleged that the sixth Earl of Anglesey had stolen his title by arranging the kidnap of the true heir. Though the titular Cloudesley participates in such a crime, he seeks to atone by raising the heir himself, and the boy undoubtedly grows into a better man under Cloudesley's guidance than he would have done as an earl. The novel's conclusion argues that love is a more significant force than either blood or wealth. All the novel's conflicts stem from the pursuit of status poisoning the wellspring of human affection, but love (familial love, respect and fraternity) is ultimately triumphant. It is arguably the weakest of Godwin's mature novels. The work contains passages of great eloquence, but the narrative itself wanders almost aimlessly (there are three stories within *Cloudesley*, but only two of them are connected) before resolving itself with relatively little excitement. Reviewers found it philosophically interesting, but dramatically inert, and even Bulwer-Lytton (writing in the *New Monthly*) was forced to concede that much of the first volume was superfluous. Before *Cloudesley* had even been published, however, Godwin was writing another collection of essays. *Thoughts on Man* (1831) is in some ways a philosophical memoir, revisiting topics covered in *Political Justice* and *The Enquirer* from nearly forty years distance. The philosopher considered it 'the most faultless book I ever printed', though perhaps few agreed – it was rejected by eleven publishers before finding a home with Effingham Wilson.[8]

Little of what Godwin had to say was new to those who had kept current with his work. At a time when parliamentary reform finally looked like a real possibility, reviewers found Godwin's criticism of secret ballots quixotic – but it was a position he had held for decades. Philosophical critics have leapt upon Godwin's reconsideration of equality at birth (i.e. the position espoused in earlier works – originally derived from Helvétius – that all human beings were born with the same potential, and that their environment made them different), but Godwin expresses this so vaguely that it appears more an idle musing than a developed position. In short, Godwin argues in *Thoughts on Man* that young people do appear to be born better disposed towards some things than others (say, languages, or mathematics, or making things) but that the details of this do not become apparent until they are more developed. Crucially, however, Godwin is firm that all young people have equal potential – it is simply a matter of allowing them to find the field in which they can excel. This obviously has political and philosophical implications, but these are fully in tune with Godwin's other positions. *Thoughts on Man* does offer the philosopher's longest discussion of gender and relationships. Godwin regards men and women as naturally equal, but argues that loving relationships (of all kinds) are based on inequality. The philosopher begins from the love of parents for their children: parents protect, teach and sacrifice for young people though there is no real benefit to the parents themselves (Godwin considers biological ties irrelevant). We love those who need us. Love between adults arises from (complementary) difference. Godwin discusses adult relationships in terms of superiors and inferiors, but also stresses that the gap between partners must not be too great (they must be on the same level to appreciate each other) encouraging us to read Godwin's idea of love as more about give and take than dominance and submission. Each partner gives of themselves to supply what the other is lacking. The philosopher's principal example of this is the relationship between Achilles and Patroclus – the famously wrathful hero in love with his companion's kindness and humanity. Godwin asserts that equals cannot fully be at peace with one another, forever uneasy at exposing their short-comings to someone so much like themselves. The philosopher argues that the inequality of loving relationships explains the development of romantic chivalry. Where the ancients simply excluded women from the public sphere, Godwin claims that medieval culture developed mutually supportive roles for men and women (women holding moral authority, men physical) that enshrined mutual deference and respect. The philosopher strikes a Burkean note here, offering no judgment on how often medieval (or contemporary) culture failed to reach this ideal. We should not, however, read this as a simple endorsement of gender roles. Godwin concludes that the purest love is based on mutual submission – and it is clear from his letters to both Wollstonecraft and Clairmont that he regarded them as his protectors as much as he was theirs.

What is most interesting about *Thoughts on Man* is its candour. Godwin's discussion of failure provides us with an insight into his thinking process – the philosopher describes enlightenment as an attempt to take control of one's own confusion, bringing what we think we know to the test again and again until it becomes clear. In a later essay, Godwin attempts to confront his own shyness and discusses the difficulty of remaining true to one's own beliefs in the face of criticism.

Thoughts on Man may not have represented many new ideas, but Godwin's old ones were still in demand. In 1830 both Godwin and Mary were approached by a breakaway publisher, Richard Bentley, looking to buy the copyrights to their most successful novels. Bentley was one of the first British publishers to make extensive use of stereotyping, allowing him to commission large print runs for minimal cost and quickly reprint if there was further demand.[9] The publisher bought the rights to *Caleb Williams*, *St Leon*, *Fleetwood* and *Frankenstein*, printing new editions of each work (Mary took the opportunity to significantly revise the text) as part of his Standard Novels series alongside the works of Jane Austen, James Fenimore Cooper and Victor Hugo. Dispensing with the wide margins and large type used by other publishers, the Standard Novels were small and affordable – *Caleb Williams* initially retailed at six shillings, a third of what it cost in 1794 – allowing Godwin's novels to reach a far larger audience than had hitherto been possible.[10]

William died in September 1832, a victim of the cholera epidemic that swept Britain that year. Godwin wrote that his son had spiralled from perfect health to death in less than four days; his parents attended him around the clock for the last two days of his life. He was twenty-nine years old. William had led a short but troubled life; Godwin's memoir describes his fiery disposition and difficulties in settling down on a career. He spent some time in prison (probably for debt) and apparently married without telling the rest of his family. He left behind a novel, *Transfusion*, which a grieving Godwin published (in 1835) with a preface describing his son's character, and which speaks to the great pride the philosopher took in the achievements of his often wayward son. The novel itself feels unfinished; the story takes a turn for the fantastic in its final chapters but ends with its best idea almost unused. Nonetheless, the work speaks to the potential that Godwin's preface describes – and is notably closer in spirit to one of Mary's novels than one of Godwin's.

Bentley published Godwin's next novel, *Deloraine*, in 1833 (though using the premium three-volume format, rather than as part of the Standard Novels series). *Deloraine* combines themes from the philosopher's most successful novels – a man on the run, an exalted first wife and a protagonist tragically consumed by jealousy regarding his second. Poignantly, the narrator of *Deloraine* is eventually saved by the efforts of his dutiful daughter. Godwin's letters imply that, when writing of the novel stalled, it was Mary's input that provided the spark to get the story moving again.[11] Father and daughter often worked in partnership in these years, proposing ideas to each other and making use of each other's publishing contacts. It was Godwin that introduced Mary to Henry Colburn, who would publish her novels *The Last Man* (1826), *Perkin Warbeck* (1830) and *Lodore* (1835).[12] Mary tried several times (unsuccessfully) to leverage her closer relationship with John Murray to her father's benefit. Mary had less need than her father to make a living by her pen, an agreement with Sir Timothy Shelley provided an allowance to support Percy Florence on condition that she published nothing controversial. This arrangement was a frequent source of grief for Mary, as Shelley's father was more than willing to see his son's literary works forgotten. Godwin and Clairmont were worse off, but they struggled along as they always had. The political climate had changed, however, and now Godwin had friends in high places.

In November 1830, the Duke of Wellington's government had been unseated by a vote of no confidence and replaced with a Whig administration led by Earl Grey. Godwin had known Grey since the politician had been a junior MP. William Lamb (Lord Melbourne) was home secretary, and Lord Brougham (who had helped Shelley with his custody battle) was Lord Chancellor. Godwin wrote regularly to them in the first few months of their government, and frequently attempted to call on them – knowing the philosopher, probably hoping to advise them on political matters. Grey's (later, Melbourne's) government stood for four years, successfully extending the right to vote with the Great Reform Act of 1832 and finally outlawing slavery across the empire in 1833. Once the government was well-established in 1832, Godwin wrote to Brougham to request a sinecure (any of the largely honorary but still salaried positions that was within the purview of an administration to grant to its supporters). Perhaps to the philosopher's surprise, his request was granted, and in 1833 Godwin was appointed to the role of office keeper and yeoman usher of the receipt of the exchequer – a job that came with £200 a year and a house in New Palace Yard. Though the position entailed little actual work, Godwin attempted to make himself useful, the sociologist Harriet Martineau wrote of him taking her on a tour of parliament and providing anecdotes from his decades of political and historical research. Asking for and accepting a sinecure was obviously a compromise – he had railed against the practice in *Political Justice* – but he probably felt the need to provide for Clairmont and knew that, in his advanced age, the government had little to gain from buying his support. The job was given out of charity, and offered the chance for Godwin to live out his last years in peace. The philosopher was at the theatre during the great fire that destroyed the Palace of Westminster in October 1834, he returned to find that Clairmont had single-handedly moved all of their books and papers to a safe location. It would be amusing to claim that the great philosophical anarchist was responsible for the destruction of parliament (the fire started from the burning of tally sticks in his department, the Exchequer) but such was Godwin's affection for the institution, he might not have seen the funny side. A few days before the fire, the position of yeoman usher had officially been abolished. Godwin had originally been told the job was for life, and he wrote nervous letters to Lord Melbourne asking him to confirm this. In the end, Melbourne was dismissed by the king before he came to decision. In the end it was the new prime minister, the Conservative Sir Robert Peel, that agreed that Godwin could stay. Peel's letter is of particular interest:

> I will not defer the assurance, that whatever I can do consistently with my public duty, to prevent a measure of Official Retrenchment from bearing hardly upon one so far advanced in years, and so distinguished by his literary character, I will do as well from a sense of Justice, as from a grateful recollection of the pleasure I have derived from those Works to which, with a just Pride, you have referred.[13]

The last work Godwin published in his lifetime was a piece of cultural history. *Lives of the Necromancers* (1834) was an investigation into people's belief in magic before the modern era. Unlike the philosopher's other histories, *Lives of the Necromancers* is well-contained, discussing

a series of isolated episodes, cases and literary texts and drawing con-
clusions from them. It is probably the most accessible of his historical
works. The work that Godwin left unfinished at the time of his death was
a collection of essays on religion under the title *The Genius of Christianity
Unveiled*. He left it to Mary to publish, as his literary executor, but it was
not printed until 1873. The essays form the philosopher's last statement
on spirituality: he declares 'a religious sense' to be essential to a healthy
mind, the ability to be awed and to accept that we as individuals are
not the centre of the universe. Religion itself, however, encroaches too
far, playing on our sense of awe (in the power of a creator) to justify
a suspension of reason (i.e. faith). Godwin argues that Christianity is
an essentially incoherent doctrine: an infinitely loving god that never-
theless threatens eternal punishment, an omniscient god that demands
formal worship in addition to a pure heart. Yet Godwin concludes that
religions are human creations that only touch on true spirituality, our
understanding of our insignificance in the totality of nature. If there is
a purpose to life, Godwin says, it is to live – 'for there is no work, nor
device, nor knowledge, nor wisdom in the grave'.[14]

Godwin recorded his meetings, reading and health until the last two
weeks of his life. The philosopher died on the evening of 7 April 1836; his
wife and daughter were by his side. He was buried alongside Wollstone-
craft in St Pancras Churchyard.

9

The Legacy

The notes that accompanied Godwin's will asked Mary to publish *The Genius of Christianity Unveiled*, but expressed a certain ambivalence about the rest of his unpublished work. His wishes were pragmatic: 'Let all that are not presently printed be consigned to the flames. But for the consideration of profit to be made, I should pass sentence of condemnation on nearly the whole ...'[1] Mary did the reverse, sitting on the religious essays while gathering her father's notes, manuscripts and letters about her in preparation to write Godwin's biography. She and Clairmont signed a contract with Henry Colburn within weeks of the philosopher's death, but the work was never completed (a rough draft of Godwin's life up to 1800 still survives). Mary turned her attentions to editing an official edition of Shelley's poems in 1838, having finally received Sir Timothy's consent. With help from her friend Caroline Norton and Edward Bulwer-Lytton, Mary helped to negotiate a pension from the Royal Bounty Fund for Clairmont until the latter's death in 1841. Percy Florence inherited the Shelley title in 1844, forever freeing Mary from financial concerns. In 1848 Percy Florence married Jane Gibson, who would go on to play an enthusiastic role in protecting the family's literary legacy.

In some ways the legacy was already well in hand. The 1832 Reform Act had done away with many of parliament's worst abuses but had not significantly extended the right to vote. The Chartist movement campaigned, much as the radicals of the 1790s had, for wider suffrage and a more democratic system of government. They appropriated Godwin's work for their own purposes: William Thomson's *Chartist Circular* (1839–42) used selective quotations from *Caleb Williams*, focusing on the protagonist's fortitude and willingness to resist. The Chartist leader Henry Vincent read *Political Justice* while imprisoned for sedition – he was tutored on it by Godwin's former ally, Francis Place – and upon leaving prison renounced direct action in favour of 'moral force' and reform through education. The same year (1841) *Caleb Williams* was serialised in John Cunningham's *Novel Newspaper*, effectively bringing the price of the novel to four pence and reaching tens of thousands of readers. A year later, the radical publisher James Watson issued a fourth edition of *Political Justice*, priced at only five shillings and made available in numbers (i.e. as a partwork) at six pence.[2]

The nascent Communist movement also took an interest in Godwin. In *The Condition of the Working Class in England* (1845) Engels declared Bentham and Godwin to be 'the two great practical philosophers of latest date' and that Godwin in particular was 'almost exclusively the property of the proletariat' – implicitly, that he believed Godwin's readers were exclusively Chartists and other working-class radicals, in contrast to Bentham's following among the 'Radical bourgeoisie'.[3] Engels privately confessed to Marx that he found Bentham tedious. In a letter regarding a planned 'library of political theory' for German activists, Engels considered the work of Charles Fourier, Henri de Saint-Simon and Robert Owen to be indispensable. Godwin failed to make the cut, principally because Engels could not support the strongly individualist conclusions of *Political Justice* (he says that Godwin regards society as 'a luxury article') but also because he saw an overlap between the arguments of *Political Justice* and Marx's (never finished) *Kritik der Politik und National-Okonomie*.[4]

Mary died in 1851, and Lady Jane Shelley exercised tight control over the Shelley-Godwin papers after her mother-in-law's death. Her own book on Shelley, *Shelley Memorials from Authentic Sources* (1859), portrays Godwin as a calming influence on the poet's wild genius, but largely omits any ideas or events that might appear controversial (thus mostly skipping the years 1814–16). The critic W. M. Rossetti alleged that Lady Jane had burned many Shelley documents that showed the poet in a bad light, and it seems apparent that (on the advice of the British Library's Richard Garnett) she trimmed or destroyed a number of letters. It seems clear that Lady Jane wanted the family to be remembered, however, and she sponsored detailed biographies of Godwin (by Charles Kegan Paul in 1876) and Shelley (by Edward Dowden in 1886) – the latter almost certainly to provide an accurate but sympathetic antidote to the many sensationalist memoirs of the poet that had emerged since his death. Kegan Paul's biography makes extensive use of Godwin's correspondence and is still a useful resource today, though it is often unclear or inaccurate on points of fact. The work displays great sympathy for Wollstonecraft, casts Clairmont in the role of wicked stepmother, and depicts the philosopher as an awkward, humourless man who attempted to live by high-minded but impractical ideals. Kegan Paul's portrait was highly influential. Dowden, however, was far less sympathetic in his assessment of Godwin. Shelley's biographer was dismissive about Godwin's ideas and considered the poet's interest in *Political Justice* 'unlucky'. Dowden's original manuscript had taken a cruelly irreverent line in discussing Godwin as a philosopher, until the family expressed their displeasure and he was encouraged to revise.[5] Dowden's guide to Godwin seems to have been the intellectual historian Sir Leslie Stephen – Stephen was nakedly hostile to Godwin's ideas, and preferred to belittle rather than engage with them. Stephen's account of the philosopher in his *History of English Thought* (1876) makes only a superficial reading of *Political Justice* before descending into ad hominem. Stephen would, however, provide the article on Godwin for the first *Dictionary of National Biography* (he was its editor from 1885 to 1891). The essay leans heavily on Kegan Paul but introduces new inaccuracies (presenting Stephen's sneering conjectures as fact) while it moralises about Godwin's dishonesty and hubris. Stephen's writing on Godwin would not have been out of place in the *Anti-Jacobin* or the *British Critic*, yet it was treated as the mainstream scholarly position.

Godwin had a new champion outside the mainstream, however. 1886 also saw the foundation of the anarchist newspaper, *Freedom*, under the editorship of Charlotte Wilson. Pyotr Alekseievich Kropotkin, Wilson's co-founder and lead writer, opened the first issue with a statement that Godwin would have approved of:

> We are socialists, disbelievers in property, advocates of the equal claims of all to work for the community as seems good – calling no-one master, and of the equal claim to each to satisfy as seems good to them, their natural needs from the stock of social wealth they have laboured to produce ... We are anarchists, disbelievers in the government of the many by the few in any shape and under any pretext.[6]

The newspaper made frequent use of Godwin in its early years. Kropotkin firmly claimed Godwin for anarchism in his 1910 essay for the *Encyclopaedia Britannica*, 'even though he did not give that name to the ideas developed in his remarkable work'.[7] For Kropotkin, as for subsequent intellectual historians such as George Woodcock, Godwin stood at the head of a long anti-authoritarian tradition. The philosopher was, however, more readily embraced by (left-wing) anarchists than (right-wing) libertarians. Kropotkin saw anarcho-communism as the natural continuation of Godwin's ideas, and identified Max Stirner as the philosopher's parallel for the individualist-anarchist school favoured by the right. Affection for Godwin's work among the anti-authoritarian left continued throughout the twentieth century: H. N. Brailsford's study *Shelley, Godwin and their Circle* (1913) is far more interested in *Political Justice* than it is the circle of Romantic poets (and may be the first critical work to stress the influence of Protestant Dissent on Godwin's early thought); Herbert Read urged a revival of Godwin's ideas in the wake of the Second World War as a counterbalance to the ever-expanding statism of its victors (Read would later influence the Green Anarchism of Murray Bookchin).[8] The philosopher's thoughts on education were a profound influence on the anarchist social historian Colin Ward, and his lectures collected as *Talking Schools* (1995) called for educationists to take note of Godwin's ideas.

Assessing Godwin's impact on (right) libertarianism is rather more difficult. Murray Rothbard, the central thinker of twentieth-century anarcho-capitalism, dismissed Godwin as a proto-Communist, yet mainstream US libertarianism commonly traces its intellectual heritage back to Thomas Jefferson – who certainly read Godwin and who, during his presidency, was satirised as the philosopher's disciple.[9] Less tenuously, Josiah Warren's concept of individual sovereignty (and rejection of 'communism') emerged from his first-hand experience of Owen's 'Community of Equality' at New Harmony, Indiana. The pivotal Benjamin Tucker (editor of the periodical *Liberty*, which published the work of individualist thinkers from both sides of the left/right divide) cited both Jefferson and Warren as key influences on his own ideas. The uniquely American individualism that originates in the transcendentalism of Henry David Thoreau (and which defies simple political categorisation) can be traced partially to Coleridge.

Godwin would probably have been gratified to see the revival of academic interest in his work in the mid-twentieth century. F. E. L. Priestley's scholarly edition of *Political Justice* (1946) made the full text readily available for the first time in nearly a century, creating the conditions for greater and greater critical attention from the 1940s up to the present day. John P. Clark was the first to write a comprehensive summary of Godwin's thought (*The Philosophical Anarchism of William Godwin*, 1977), clarifying the philosopher's positions on a variety of issues through reference to the entire body of his work. Mark Philp, in *Godwin's Political Justice* (1986), drilled down into all three editions of the treatise to identify what are now accepted as the work's core principles (the ideas that remain consistent across all versions of the text) and attempting to explain the thinking behind Godwin's revisions. Philp also led the project that digitised Godwin's diary, making it possible to cross reference nearly forty years of his social engagements, reading, writing, and private events. In the twenty-first century the reappraisal of Godwin's novels and his influence on period fiction has been led by Pamela Clemit and Tilottama Rajan, resulting in a new generation of critics looking closely at novels other than *Caleb Williams* (Clemit has also been instrumental in publishing the philosopher's correspondence). Godwin has been the subject of three comprehensive biographies: by Don Locke (1980), Peter Marshall (1984, revised 2017) and William St Clair (1989); each has its own merits.

The philosopher has, for a century or more, been overshadowed by the rest of his family. Without wishing to diminish the vital contribution of Wollstonecraft to feminism, or of the Shelleys to literature, this imbalance has done Godwin a disservice and (until recent years) ignored his place at the centre of English Romanticism. Not only should we take note of Godwin as a novelist and political thinker, but also consider his pioneering work as a historian and children's publisher. In both fields, Godwin's work was ahead of its time. The philosopher's ideas on education, long neglected, were arrived at independently by progressive educationists in the mid-twentieth century; his theory of reading appears to be borne out by modern cognitive psychology. Godwin's ideas remain challenging, however. The philosopher envisions the eventual demise of authority, not through its revolutionary overthrow, but because of its ultimate irrelevance to a post-scarcity society. Godwin argues that a society that values individual judgment has unlimited scope for progress. By contrast, the more a community seeks to manage its people the more it gradually diminishes them. The philosopher's ideas would be demanding even if they did not question some of the basic principles the states we live in are founded upon, but we should take heart from Godwin's own continual return to his own works in search of clarity and accuracy.

As we have seen, Godwin revised many of his major works, not only to better express his thoughts, but because those thoughts had been reconsidered and themselves revised. The philosopher considered this essential to serious intellectual endeavour, though it brought him criticism from contemporaries (both friend and foe). Godwin's detractors have frequently leapt on his revisions as if the philosopher had in some way surrendered, sometimes ignoring that his new position was as much a challenge to convention as his old one. Critical friends (Shelley among them) sometimes lamented the qualification of his most challenging or controversial ideas – Godwin was always the first to recognise that big ideas were usually also complex ones, and he refused to sacrifice accuracy for the sake of rhetoric. The philosopher might have been amused at how much ink has been spilled over the search for consistency in his work, arguing that 'the active and independent mind, the genuine lover of and enquirer after truth, will inevitably pass through certain revolutions of opinion'.[10] Some core principles remain consistent throughout his work however: the duty to act according to private judgment, the value of conversation as both a critical tool and source of education, and the importance of empathy to moral action. The philosopher subjected his own work to rigorous examination – the threads that remain consistent are the most robust.

It is not uncommon to read in Godwin scholarship the opinion that such and such a revision causes the collapse of his whole system. This assumes that the philosopher was an architect of systems. Few, if any, of Godwin's works seek to offer a comprehensive account of their subject – *Political Justice* is his most systematic, but it remains an enquiry (an investigation) rather than a manifesto, focused on exploding the intellectual and moral contradictions of political society while only speculating on the possible gains of doing differently. Other works make suggestions, but further works question them. Some have regarded Godwin's career as a steady retreat from the boldness of the arguments he advanced in the 1790s, Godwin himself saw his revisions as improvements. For all his occasional pomposity, the philosopher could acknowledge his own shortcomings and was receptive to honest criticism. In *The Enquirer*, Godwin wrote that for an adult to (ethically) gain the confidence of a child was difficult and that one should expect to fail. The sentiment could be extended to describe the philosopher's approach to any worthwhile venture: we should attempt to do the right thing and expect to get it wrong. Even when we think we are successful, we must examine our conclusions – discuss those conclusions with others – and expect to find holes and mistakes in our work. But we must persevere:

> It is the characteristic of ordinary minds to fly from one scheme to the other. It is the characteristic of genius, though it fall, to rise again, though it suffer defeats to persist, and though obliged to alter and modify many of its judgments, never to part with that clearness of spirit which attended their formation.[11]

Such is the progressive nature of humanity. Godwin did not subscribe to notions of inexorable improvement, the betterment of humanity was in his view contingent on our ability to foster critical reason and empathy in future generations. His writing stands as testament to that, both his great works and his little ones. His life was full of failures too, mistakes and compromises that we might fairly criticise him for. Yet after every failure, the philosopher was back at his desk writing something new – rising again, hoping to awaken genius.

Notes

The following abbreviations are used in the notes that follow for brevity:

CNMG   *The Collected Novels and Memoirs of William Godwin*, edited by Pamela Clemit, Mark Philp and Maurice Hindle, 8 volumes (London: Pickering, 1992).

PPWG   *Political and Philosophical Writings of William Godwin*, edited by Mark Philp, Pamela Clemit and Martin Fitzpatrick, 7 volumes (London: Pickering, 1993).

Letters   *The Letters of William Godwin*, edited by Pamela Clemit, 2 volumes to date (Oxford: Oxford University Press, 2011).

Chapter 2

1. *CNMG*, vol. 1, p. 10.
2. Ibid., p. 30.
3. Ibid., p. 37.
4. Ibid., p. 31.
5. Ibid., p. 36.
6. Ibid., p. 42.
7. Autobiographical note, Abinger Collection, c.32, folio 34. The Abinger Collection, held at the Bodleian Library, comprises the correspondence and papers of three generations of the Godwin/Shelley family (hereafter referred to as 'MS Abinger').
8. *CNMG*, vol. 1, p. 53.
9. Godwin liked to depict himself as a man of logic and reason, a description that critics and biographers took at face value and later amplified. Godwin's first twentieth-century biographer, Ford K. Brown, insisted that Godwin was 'painfully devoid of humour and of taste' (*The Life of William Godwin*, London: J. M. Dent & Sons, 1926, p. 33). In contrast, his writing regularly displays notes of whimsy that do not chime with the later caricature.
10. To the theatre historian William Dunlap, quoted in Dunlap, *A History of the American Theatre* (New York: J & J Harper, 1832), p. 182.
11. Charles Kegan Paul, *William Godwin, His Friends and Contemporaries* (London: Henry S. King & Co., 1876), vol. 1, p. 61.

12. Price, *Discourse on the Love of Our Country* (London: T. Cadell, 1789), p. 40.
13. Ibid., p. 50.
14. Letter, n.d., MS Abinger, c.17, folio 29.
15. William Godwin, *Of Population* (London: Longman, Hurst, Bees, Orme and Brown, 1820), p. iv.

Chapter 3

1. Mary Shelley reported her father's account of (then prime minister) Pitt the Younger's opinion that, 'a three guinea book could never do much harm among those who had not three shillings to spare'. Pamela Clemit and A. A. Markley (eds), *Mary Shelley's Literary Lives and Other Writings* (London: Routledge, 2002), vol. 4, p. 86.
2. William Hazlitt, *Spirit of the Age* in *Complete Works of William Hazlitt*, ed. P. P. Howe (London: J. M. Dent and Sons, 1930–4), vol. 11, p. 17.
3. *PPWG*, vol. 3, p. 50.
4. Ibid., p. 51.
5. Ibid., p. 75.
6. Ibid., p. 95.
7. Ibid., p. 231.
8. Ibid., p. 240.
9. Ibid., p. 250.
10. Ibid., p. 253.
11. Ibid., p. 289.
12. Ibid., p. 307.
13. Ibid., p. 377.
14. Ibid., pp. 374–5.
15. Ibid., p. 423.
16. Ibid., p. 457.
17. Ibid., p. 453.
18. Though present in English common law for centuries, the widespread recognition of coverture as a legal principle is thought to stem from William Blackstone's *Commentaries on the Laws of England* (1765–9). Godwin's diary records his use of Blackstone throughout his research for *Political Justice*.
19. *PPWG*, vol. 3, p. 453.
20. Ibid., p. 454.
21. The philosopher is pulling ideas out of the air, at this point. Godwin is, to some extent, right: estimates today place the world population at under one billion for much of his life – but demography was poorly understood

at the time, and reliable data largely absent. The first modern census of Britain was conducted in 1801.

Chapter 4

1. *CNMG*, vol. 3, p. 4.
2. For a novel, a conservative first printing in the period was usually 500 copies. An established author with a recent success behind him may have warranted an initial print run twice that size. *Caleb Williams* went to a second and third edition before the end of the decade (we lack numbers for either of them), so it seems likely that the novel sold several thousand copies in only a few years. To put these numbers in context, Sir Walter Scott's novel *Waverley* (1814), one of the best-selling novels of the period, sold around 40,000 copies in Scott's lifetime.
3. MS Abinger, c.38, folio 2.
4. Godwin does not directly address why this should be, but we can infer his position from his theory of knowledge as it appears in the revised *Political Justice*. Proper intellectual rigour insists that we consider every situation as a case in itself, without allowing our prior experiences (perhaps, prejudices) to cloud our judgment. Yet we are unlikely to ever have the full picture of a situation, and past experience can fill in many of the gaps (X has always been true in the past, and it explains Y). We are inclined to look for heuristics to help us make quick judgments: acting with benevolence seems likely to increase happiness, so it supplies a 'good' answer, if not necessarily the 'correct' one (which, all other things being uncertain, may be impossible to ascertain). Experience may come to reinforce this. We ultimately come to value benevolence as good, rather than the effects of benevolence.
5. John Barrell, *Imagining the King's Death: Figurative Treason, Fantasies of Regicide 1793–1796* (Oxford: Oxford University Press, 2000), p. 553.
6. *The True Briton* was one of a number of periodicals founded or supported by government money around this time. *The Sun* and *The True Briton* were daily newspapers operated by the government pamphleteer John Heriot. The *British Critic* and William Gifford's *Anti-Jacobin* were literary journals that published reactionary satire and hostile reviews of books that strayed from the conservative line of church, king, and family values. For more on this, see John Barrell, *Imagining the King's Death* and Kevin Gilmartin, *Writing Against Revolution: Literary Conservatism in Britain 1790–1832* (Cambridge: Cambridge University Press, 2007).
7. *PPWG*, vol. 2, p. 149.
8. *Letters*, vol. 1, p. 138.

Chapter 5

1. *CNMG*, vol. 1, p. 112.
2. Ibid., p. 110.
3. Ibid., p. 122.
4. Ibid.
5. Godwin to Mary Wollstonecraft, 13 July 1796, in *Letters*, vol. 1, p. 171.
6. Wollstonecraft to William Godwin, 17 August 1796, in Mary Wollstonecraft, *Collected Letters of Mary Wollstonecraft*, edited by Ralph M. Wardle (Ithaca, NY: Cornell University Press, 1979), pp. 336–7 (hereafter referred to as '*Letters of Wollstonecraft*').
7. Godwin to Mary Wollstonecraft, 17 August 1796, in *Letters*, vol. 1, pp. 173–4.
8. *PPWG*, vol. 5, p. 107.
9. Godwin to Thomas Wedgwood, 19 April 1797, in *Letters*, vol. 1, p. 199.
10. *CNMG*, vol. 1, p. 130.
11. Godwin to Mary Hays, 10 April 1797, in *Letters*, vol. 1, p. 197.
12. She may have principally meant religion. Wollstonecraft was a believer – she had been a member of Richard Price's congregation at Newington Green – while Godwin at the time still regarded himself as an atheist. Wollstonecraft to Amelia Alderson, 11 April 1797, in *Letters of Wollstonecraft*, p. 389.
13. Wollstonecraft to Godwin, 21 May 1797, in *Letters of Wollstonecraft*, p. 394.
14. Wollstonecraft to Godwin, 19 June 1797, ibid., pp. 398–9.
15. *CNMG*, vol. 1. p. 135.
16. Ibid., p. 117.
17. Ibid., p. 129.
18. Roscoe papers MS 3958A.
19. The most successful of these, Isaac D'Israeli's *Vaurien* (1797), may have amused Wollstonecraft with its depiction – she wrote a note to Godwin that read, 'There is a good boy write me a review …' (17 March 1797). Caricatures of Godwin, Wollstonecraft, and many of their friends, appeared in conservative and reactionary fiction throughout the period. The book historian M. O. Grenby attempts to align some of these characters with real-life personages in *The Anti-Jacobin Novel* (Cambridge: Cambridge University Press, 2001), pp. 226–7.
20. Malthus, *Essay on the Principle of Population*, 1st edition, in E. A. Wrigley and David Souden (eds), *The Works of Thomas Robert Malthus*, vol. 1 (London: Routledge, 1986), ch. 10.
21. Malthus to Godwin, 20 August 1798, quoted in *Letters*, vol. 2.
22. Godwin to James Mackintosh, January 1799, ibid.
23. Mackintosh to Godwin, January 1799, quoted in ibid., p. 71.

24. Unaddressed letter, June or July 1799, ibid., pp. 83–4.
25. Godwin to George Robinson, 14 September 1799, ibid.
26. William Maginn, 'William Godwin', in 'A Gallery of Illustrious Literary Characters', no. 53, *Fraser's Magazine*, 10 (October 1834), p. 463.
27. *CNMG*, vol. 4, p. 270.

Chapter 6

1. Coleridge to John Thelwall, 13 May 1796, in Earl Leslie Griggs (ed.), *Collected Letters of Samuel Taylor Coleridge*, 6 volumes (Oxford: Oxford University Press, 1956), vol. 1, p. 215. See also *The Friend* in Barbara E. Rooke (ed.), *The Collected Works of Samuel Taylor Coleridge*, 16 volumes (Princeton, NJ: Princeton University Press, 1969), vol. 4, p. 334–8.
2. Coleridge to Godwin, 29 March 1811, ibid., vol. 3, p. 315.
3. Godwin knew Frend well, the two were both frequently dinner guests of Horne Tooke. Frend had been connected romantically with Mary Hays, and her novel *Memoirs of Emma Courtney* (1796) draws on the experience – Godwin appears in the novel as Emma's mentor, Mr Francis.
4. *CNMG*, vol. 1, p. 53.
5. *Letters of Charles and Mary Lamb*, vol. 1, p. 185.
6. In the poem 'Living without God in the World' (in Robert Southey's *Annual Anthology* the previous year) the poet wrote that, 'Some braver spirits of a modern stamp/Affect a Godhead nearer ...'. This is discussed in detail in Felicity James, *Charles Lamb, Coleridge and Wordsworth: Reading Friendship in the 1790s* (Basingstoke: Palgrave Macmillan, 2008), pp. 134–6.
7. Reported by Robert Southey in C. C. Southey (ed.), *The Life and Correspondence of Robert Southey* (New York: Harper, 1851), p. 536–7.
8. Charles Lamb to Thomas Manning, August 1801, in Edwin W. Marrs (ed.), *Letters of Charles and Mary Lamb* (Ithaca, NY: Cornell University Press, 1976), vol. 1, p. 230.
9. Samuel Parr, *A Spital Sermon, preached at Christ Church, upon Easter Tuesday, April 15, 1800, to Which are Added Notes* (London: J. Mawman, 1801), p. 4.
10. Godwin to Samuel Parr, 24 April 1800, in *Letters*, vol. 2, p. 201.
11. 'Pray come & see me – I admire your Talents – I love your Philanthropy – I am ambitious of your friendship'. Parr to Godwin, 4 September 1794, MS Abinger, c.2, folio 47.
12. Parr to Godwin, 29 April 1800, MS Abinger, c.5, folios 113–18.
13. MS Abinger, c.21, folio 61.
14. Parr, *Spital Sermon*, p. 52.
15. *PPWG*, vol. 2, p. 165.

16. Ibid., pp. 170–1.
17. Ibid., p. 171.
18. Ibid., p. 177.
19. Ibid., p. 178.
20. Ibid., p. 190.
21. Ibid., pp. 190–1.
22. Ibid., p. 198.
23. Reproduced in ibid., pp. 211–3.
24. This addition remained part of Malthus's *Essay* even in its final, definitive edition in 1826. See Wrigley and Souden, *Works of Thomas Robert Malthus*, vol. 3, p. 55.
25. Exact publication figures for *Caleb Williams* are unclear, though it was obviously a resounding success for its first two publishers. For context, *St Leon*'s initial print run of a thousand copies sold out in less than two months but the novel did not reach a third printing until 1816.
26. For more on theatre audiences, see W. Van Lennep et al. (eds) *The London Stage 1660–1800* (Carbondale, IL: Southern Illinois University Press, 1968). Novel buying and circulating libraries are discussed at length in William St Clair, *The Reading Nation in the Romantic Period* (Cambridge: Cambridge University Press, 2004), which also contains significant information on the early publication history of both Godwin and Mary Shelley's work.
27. Charles Lamb, 'The Old Actors', *London Magazine*, April 1822, in E. V. Lucas (ed.), *The Works of Charles and Mary Lamb*, vol. 2 (New York: AMS Press, 1968), pp. 292–3.
28. See Vicki Parslow Stafford, 'Claire Clairmont, Mary Jane's Daughter: New Correspondence with Claire's Father', retrieved from https://sites.google.com/site/maryjanesdaughter.
29. For more on this, see Hubert Huscher, 'The Clairmont Enigma' in *Keats–Shelley Memorial Bulletin*, XI (1960), pp. 10–16; and William St Clair, *The Godwins and the Shelleys: The Biography of a Family* (London: Faber & Faber, 1989), pp. 248–54.
30. Godwin to unknown addressee, February or March 1801, in *Letters*, vol. 2, p. 209–10.
31. The 'Chaucer house' had been owned by the poet's son, Sir Thomas Chaucer in the fifteenth century. Godwin's letter tells us that the author believed his subject had resided there at some point, but there is no evidence of this. Godwin to Mary Jane Godwin, 9 October 1801, in *Letters*, vol. 2, pp. 241–4.
32. Godwin, *Life of Chaucer* (London: Richard Phillips, 1803), vol. 1, p. xix.
33. Ibid., p. 370.
34. *PPWG*, vol. 5, pp. 313–4.

35. *CNMG*, vol. 5, p. 13.
36. Quoted in a letter by Godwin explaining the situation to Marshall the same day (the year appears to have been wrong in Holcroft's original), 28 February 1805, in *Letters*, vol. 2, p. 338.
37. Godwin, *Fables Ancient and Modern, Volume 1*, ed. Suzanne L. Barnett and Katherine Bennett Gustafson (College Park, MD: Romantic Circles, University of Maryland, 2014; retrieved from www.rc.umd.edu/editions/godwin_fables/index.html), vol. 1, paras 292–3.
38. Coleridge to Southey, 1799, in Coleridge, *Collected Letters*, vol. 1, p. 553.
39. Godwin to Dr Edward Ash, 21 May 1808, MS Abinger, c.10, folios 64–5.
40. The account of Holcroft's final days comes from Hazlitt's *Life of Thomas Holcroft*, ed. Elbridge Colby (New York: Benjamin Bloom, 1968), vol. 2, p. 310.
41. Godwin to Louisa Holcroft, undated, MS Abinger, c.19, folio 17b.
42. MS Abinger, c.19, folio 17b.
43. *PPWG*, vol. 3, p. 137.
44. Godwin to Mary Jane Godwin, 21 August 1809, MS Abinger, c.42, folio 40.

Chapter 7

1. From an account of Godwin and Shelley by Place (B. M. Add. MSS. 3, 145, 30–36) quoted in Walter Peck, *Shelley: His Life and Work*, vol. 2 (London: Ernest Benn, 1927), p. 416. In the manuscript, the criticism of Clairmont is crossed out in pencil, probably by Place's son, who edited his father's papers for publication.
2. 'A Greybeard's Gossip about a Literary Acquaintance' in *New Monthly Magazine* (1848).
3. *PPWG*, vol. 5, p. 174.
4. Godwin to Mary Jane Godwin, 18 May 1811, quoted in Kegan Paul, vol. 2, p. 182.
5. Percy Shelley to Godwin, 3 January 1812, in Frederick L. Jones (ed.), *The Letters of Percy Bysshe Shelley, Vol. 1: Shelley in England* (Oxford: Oxford University Press, 1964), pp. 220–1 (hereafter referred to as '*Letters of Shelley*').
6. Percy Shelley to Godwin, 10 January 1812, ibid., pp. 227–9.
7. The quotation is from the *Merchant of Venice*, IV.i., ll. 73–7. Letter, Godwin to Percy Shelley, 4 March 1812, *CNMG*, vol. 1, p. 70.
8. Godwin to Percy Shelley, 14 March 1812, ibid., p. 74.
9. Godwin to Percy Shelley, 30 March 1812, ibid., p. 77.
10. Godwin to Percy Shelley, 4 March 1812, ibid., p. 72.

11. We can infer further details of these conversations based on Godwin's philosophical interests. Matter and spirit probably refers to a discussion of Berkeley and scepticism, as an unpublished essay of Godwin's shows the philosopher to be in tune with his predecessor's position on our perception of the physical world. Shelley's 'atheism' is principally a rejection of organised religion and, like Godwin, expressed religious views that could be described as pantheist. Utility and truth probably relate to the ethics of *Political Justice*, which in turn implies that 'party' refers to Godwin's critique of political factionalism in the same work. Their discussion of the church may be a topical conversation, or relate to the episcopal conflicts of the seventeenth century (including the English Civil War) which later became one of Godwin's major historical interests. 'Germanism' is a reference to gothic fiction – the most lurid works of the period often traded on some German connection, imitating the *Schauerromane* (shudder novels) of central Europe, and the phrase became synonymous with the genre as a whole. Godwin read one of Shelley's gothic romances (*St Irvyne; or, The Rosicrucian*) in June that year.

12. The Shelley family had only come by their baronetcy in 1806 and the poet's father was keen to maintain a respectable front. Harriet was a lower-middle-class school friend of Shelley's sister; the couple had eloped together in 1811.

13. Godwin to John Taylor, 27 August 1814, *Letters of Shelley*, vol. 1, p. 390, n. 3.

14. Mary Jane Godwin to Lady Mountcashell, 20 August 1814, quoted in Edward Dowden, *The Life of Percy Bysshe Shelley* (London: Kegan Paul, Trench, 1886), vol. 2, appendix A, p. 544.

15. Quoted in Don Locke, *A Fantasy of Reason* (London: Routledge & Kegan Paul, 1980), p. 138.

16. Percy Shelley to Harriet Shelley, 27 September 1814, *Letters of Shelley*, vol. 1, p. 398.

17. Mary Godwin to Percy Shelley, 28 October 1814, ibid., p. 414, n. 4.

18. Godwin to John Taylor, 27 August 1814, held in the Huntington Library in San Marino, California. The first section is quoted in *Letters of Shelley*, vol. 1, p. 390, n. 3; the second, in William St Clair, *The Godwins and the Shelleys*, p. 367.

19. Mary Wollstonecraft Shelley (née Godwin) in Paula R. Feldman and Diana Scott-Kilvert (eds), *The Journals of Mary Shelley, 1814–1844*, Journal Book I, vol. 1 (Oxford: Oxford University Press, 1987).

20. Percy Shelley to William Godwin, 6 March 1816, in *Letters of Shelley*, vol. 1, p. 459.

21. Scott, who had written irreverent and dismissive reviews of so many of Godwin's books, later contributed money to a public subscription for

Godwin (though he asked his name not be recorded) out of respect for his talents, though he said he could not condone his opinions.

22. Percy Shelley to William Godwin, 3 May 1816, in *Letters of Shelley*, vol. 1, pp. 472–3.

23. Percy Shelley to William Godwin, 2 October 1816, ibid., p. 509.

24. Fanny Godwin to Mary Godwin, 3 October 1816, ibid., p. 509, n. 2.

25. Quoted in Kegan Paul, vol. 2, p. 242.

26. Percy Shelley to Mary Godwin, 16 December 1816, in *Letters of Shelley*, vol. 1, p. 520.

27. Scholars have argued that Clairmont was prone to distort the truth as an exercise in damage limitation, attempting to deflect criticism of the family by offering more palatable versions of events to lessen the scandal. Not all of her accounts make sense in this light, however, as Mary Jane frequently gave inaccurate dates, or attributed actions to different people, for no readily apparent reason. Mostly famously, Clairmont told Lady Mountcashell that it was Marshall that pursued the trio to Calais in 1814, rather than herself. It is usually asserted that she did this to evade blame for failing to recover them, but since the story she gave did not flatter her either, this seems a curious piece of deception.

28. Percy Shelley to Claire Clairmont, 30 December 1816, in *Letters of Shelley*, vol. 1, p. 525.

29. Mary published a substantially revised edition in 1831, and the later text is the version more familiar to modern readers. The 1831 novel irons out some of the original's ambiguities; Walton is seen to learn from Victor's hubris, and the author removes any reference to Elizabeth and Victor being blood relatives.

30. Place, quoted in Locke, *A Fantasy of Reason*, p. 238.

31. Godwin to Percy Shelley, 31 January 1818, quoted in *Letters of Shelley*, vol. 1, p. 597.

32. Godwin to Mary Shelley, 27 October 1818, MS Abinger, c.52, folio 13.

33. Godwin to Mary Shelley, 9 September 1819, MS Abinger, c.45, folio 18.

34. Shelley asserted that he did this with Mary's consent, but the poet's letters are not always a complete account.

Chapter 8

1. Godwin to Caroline Lamb, 25 February 1819, MS Abinger, c.12, folio 43.

2. If this was the case, then Godwin was unsuccessful – Scarlett became increasingly conservative in later years, becoming an ally of the Duke of Wellington against parliamentary reform. He became Baron Abinger in 1835. Ironically, Percy Florence Shelley's adopted daughter, Bessie,

married Scarlett's grandson and the Abinger family eventually inherited the combined Shelley–Godwin papers (now held at the Bodleian Library).

3. Godwin to Clairmont, 31 August 1819, MS Abinger, c.43, folios 4–5.

4. See Drew R. McCoy, 'Jefferson and Madison on Malthus: Population Growth in Jeffersonian Political Economy' in *The Virginia Magazine of History and Biography*, 88(3) (July 1980), pp. 259–76.

5. Thomas Robert Malthus, *Edinburgh Review*, 35 (1821), quoted in Kenneth W. Graham (ed.), *William Godwin Reviewed: A Reception History 1783–1834* (New York: AMS Press, 2001), p. 392.

6. Mary Shelley to Leigh Hunt, 11 September 1823, in Betty T. Bennett (ed.), *Letters of Mary Wollstonecraft Shelley*, vol. 1 (Baltimore, MD: Johns Hopkins University Press, 1980), p. 378.

7. It was common practice for theatres to 'steal' popular novels by making enough changes to claim that copyright had not been violated. George Colman had done exactly this with *Caleb Williams*, though he did compensate Godwin with free entry to the Haymarket for years afterwards.

8. The quotation comes from his notes for Mary on what to do with his notes and unpublished writing (written 1834). MS Abinger, c.38, folio 13.

9. Stereotyping is the process of casting whole pages as printing plates, rather than using moveable type to assemble pages one at a time. Stereotyping required a significant initial investment (making the plates) but became more profitable the more copies were sold – British publishers had previously only used the technology to produce books for which there was perennial demand (Bibles, textbooks) – so Bentley's offer displayed confidence in Godwin's sales potential.

10. The impact of this wider readership would become apparent after the author's death. Both *Caleb Williams* and *Frankenstein* remained in print until the end of the series in the mid-1850s, indicating consistent sales as Bentley gradually cut prices (by the time it went out of print, *Frankenstein* sold at 2s 6d), but the publisher never cut to the level that would have facilitated the enormous popularity of Scott or Byron (the works of both were readily available in sixpenny editions by the Victorian era).

11. Godwin to Mary Shelley, 13 April 1832, in Jane Shelley (ed.), *Shelley and Mary* (privately printed, c. 1882; a copy is held at the Bodleian Library), vol. 4, pp. 1161–2.

12. Godwin helped to research *Perkin Warbeck* at the British Museum, as we can see in his letters of the 13 August 1828, 29 May 1829 and 30 May 1829; *Shelley and Mary*, iv, pp. 1106C–D, 1122A–B.

13. Sir Robert Peel to Godwin, 9 February 1835, quoted in Locke, *A Fantasy of Reason*, p. 338.

14. *PPWG*, vol. 7, p. 233.

Chapter 9

1. Note dated 30 June 1834, MS Abinger, c.38, folio 13.

2. The impact of Watson's edition is hard to measure. No information has been found regarding its sales or the size of its print run, nor is there an identifiable surge in the public discussion of *Political Justice* (references in newspapers, for example) that might suggest a significantly expanded readership.

3. Friedrich Engels, *The Condition of the Working Class in England*, in *Marx/Engels Collected Works*, vol. 4 (London: Lawrence and Wishart, 1975), p. 528.

4. Friedrich Engels to Karl Marx, 17 March 1845, in *Marx/Engels Collected Works*, vol. 38 (London: Lawrence and Wishart, 1982), p. 27.

5. Edward Dowden to Richard Garnett, 25 May 1885, in R. S. Garnett (ed.), *Letters About Shelley: Interchanged by Three Friends – Edward Dowden, Richard Garnett and Wm. Michael Rossetti* (London: Hodder and Stoughton, 1917), pp. 113–14.

6. Kropotkin, *Freedom*, 1(1) (October 1886). The journal continues to this day as an online publication (http://freedomnews.org.uk) and carries this passage as a strapline at the bottom of the page.

7. Kropotkin, 'Anarchism', in the *Encyclopaedia Britannica*, 11th edition (New York: Encyclopaedia Britannica, 1910), vol. 1, p. 915.

8. Herbert Read, preface to George Woodcock's *William Godwin: A Biographical Study* (London: Porcupine Press, 1946), p. xi.

9. See Charles O. Lerche, Jr. 'Jefferson and the Election of 1800: A Case Study in the Political Smear', in *The William and Mary Quarterly*, 5(4) (October 1948), pp. 467–91; and Burton R. Pollin, 'Godwin's Letter to Ogilvie, Friend of Jefferson, and the Federalist Propaganda', in *Journal of the History of Ideas*, 28(3) (July–September 1967), pp. 432–44.

10. *PPWG*, vol. 5, p. 295.

11. Godwin to James Ogilvie, n.d. 1797, published in the *Washington National Intelligencer* (16 April 1802).

Bibliography

Barrell, John. *Imagining the King's Death: Figurative Treason, Fantasies of Regicide 1793–1796* (Oxford: Oxford University Press, 2000).

Brailsford, H. N. *Shelley, Godwin and their Circle* (London: Williams & Norgate, 1913).

Brown, Ford K. *The Life of William Godwin* (London: J. M. Dent & Sons, 1926).

Clark, John P. *The Philosophical Anarchism of William Godwin* (Princeton, NJ: Princeton University Press, 1977).

Clemit, Pamela and A. A. Markley (eds). *Mary Shelley's Literary Lives and Other Writings* (London: Routledge, 2002).

Coleridge, Samuel Taylor. *Collected Letters of Samuel Taylor Coleridge*, 6 volumes, ed. Earl Leslie Griggs (Oxford: Oxford University Press, 1956).

Coleridge, Samuel Taylor. *The Collected Works of Samuel Taylor Coleridge*, 16 volumes, ed. Barbara E. Rooke (Princeton, NJ: Princeton University Press, 1969).

Dowden, Edward. *The Life of Percy Bysshe Shelley* (London: Kegan Paul, Trench, 1886).

Dunlap, William. *A History of the American Theatre* (New York: J. & J. Harper, 1832).

Engels, Friedrich. *The Condition of the Working Class in England*, in *Marx/Engels Collected Works*, vol. 4 (London: Lawrence and Wishart, 1975).

Garnett, R. S. (ed.). *Letters About Shelley: Interchanged by Three Friends – Edward Dowden, Richard Garnett and Wm. Michael Rossetti* (London: Hodder and Stoughton, 1917).

Gilmartin, Kevin. *Writing Against Revolution: Literary Conservatism in Britain 1790–1832* (Cambridge: Cambridge University Press, 2007).

Godwin, William, *The Collected Novels and Memoirs of William Godwin*, edited by Pamela Clemit, Mark Philp and Maurice Hindle, 8 volumes (London: Pickering, 1992).

Godwin, William. *Fables Ancient and Modern, Volume 1*, ed. Suzanne L. Barnett and Katherine Bennett Gustafson (College Park, MD: Romantic Circles, University of Maryland, 2014; retrieved from www.rc.umd.edu/editions/godwin_fables/index.html).

Godwin, William, *The Letters of William Godwin*, edited by Pamela Clemit, 2 volumes to date (Oxford: Oxford University Press, 2011).

Godwin, William. *Life of Chaucer* (London: Richard Phillips, 1803).

Godwin, William. *Of Population* (London: Longman, Hurst, Bees, Orme and Brown, 1820).

Godwin, William, *Political and Philosophical Writings of William Godwin*, edited by Mark Philp, Pamela Clemit and Martin Fitzpatrick, 7 volumes (London: Pickering, 1993).

Godwin, William. *Political Justice*, ed. F. E. L. Priestley (Toronto: University of Toronto Press, 1946).

Graham, Kenneth W. (ed.). *William Godwin Reviewed: A Reception History 1783–1834* (New York: AMS Press, 2001).

Hazlitt, William. *Complete Works of William Hazlitt*, ed. P. P. Howe (London: J. M. Dent and Sons, 1930–4).

Hazlitt, William. *Life of Thomas Holcroft*, ed. Elbridge Colby (New York: Benjamin Bloom, 1968).

Huscher, Hubert. 'The Clairmont Enigma', in *Keats–Shelley Memorial Bulletin*, XI (1960), pp. 10–16.

James, Felicity. *Charles Lamb, Coleridge and Wordsworth: Reading Friendship in the 1790s* (Basingstoke: Palgrave Macmillan, 2008).

Jones, Frederick L. (ed.). *The Letters of Percy Bysshe Shelley, Vol. 1: Shelley in England* (Oxford: Oxford University Press, 1964).

Kegan Paul, Charles. *William Godwin, His Friends and Contemporaries* (London: Henry S. King & Co., 1876).

Lamb, Charles, and Mary Lamb. *Letters of Charles and Mary Lamb*, ed. Edwin W. Marrs (Ithaca, NY: Cornell University Press, 1976).

Lamb, Charles, and Mary Lamb. *The Works of Charles and Mary Lamb*, vol. 2, ed. E. V. Lucas (New York: AMS Press, 1968).

Lerche, Jr., Charles O. 'Jefferson and the Election of 1800: A Case Study in the Political Smear', in *The William and Mary Quarterly*, 5(4) (October 1948), pp. 467–91.

Locke, Don. *A Fantasy of Reason* (London: Routledge & Kegan Paul, 1980).

Maginn, William. 'William Godwin', in 'A Gallery of Illustrious Literary Characters', no. 53, *Fraser's Magazine*, 10 (October 1834), p. 463.

Malthus, Thomas. *Essay on the Principle of Population*, 1st edition, in *The Works of Thomas Robert Malthus*, vol. 1, ed. E. A. Wrigley and David Souden (London: Routledge, 1986), ch. 10.

Marshall, Peter. *William Godwin: Philosopher, Novelist, Revolutionary* (Oakland, CA: PM Press, 2017).

McCoy, Drew R. 'Jefferson and Madison on Malthus: Population Growth in Jeffersonian Political Economy', in *The Virginia Magazine of History and Biography*, 88(3) (July 1980), pp. 259–76.

Mellor, Anne K. *Mary Shelley: Her Life, Her Fiction, Her Monsters* (New York: Routledge, 1989).

Parr, Samuel. *A Spital Sermon, preached at Christ Church, upon Easter Tuesday, April 15, 1800, to Which are Added Notes* (London: J. Mawman, 1801).

Peck, Walter. *Shelley: His Life and Work*, vol. 2 (London: Ernest Benn, 1927).

Philp, Mark. *Godwin's Political Justice* (London: Duckworth, 1986).

Pollin, Burton R. 'Godwin's Letter to Ogilvie, Friend of Jefferson, and the Federalist Propaganda', in *Journal of the History of Ideas*, 28(3) (July–September 1967), pp. 432–44.

Price, Richard. *Discourse on the Love of Our Country* (London: T. Cadell, 1789).

St Clair, William. *The Godwins and the Shelleys: The Biography of a Family* (London: Faber & Faber, 1989).

St Clair, William. *The Reading Nation in the Romantic Period* (Cambridge: Cambridge University Press, 2004).

Shelley, Jane (ed.). *Shelley and Mary* (privately printed, c. 1882; a copy is held at the Bodleian Library).

Shelley, Mary. *The Journals of Mary Shelley, 1814–1844*, ed. Paula R. Feldman and Diana Scott-Kilvert (Oxford: Oxford University Press, 1987).

Shelley, Mary. *Letters of Mary Wollstonecraft Shelley*, ed. Betty T. Bennett, vol. 1 (Baltimore, MD: Johns Hopkins University Press, 1980).

Southey, C. C. (ed.). *The Life and Correspondence of Robert Southey* (New York: Harper, 1851).

Stafford, Vicki Parslow. 'Claire Clairmont, Mary Jane's Daughter: New Correspondence with Claire's Father', retrieved from https://sites.google.com/site/maryjanesdaughter.

Todd, Janet. *Mary Wollstonecraft: A Revolutionary Life* (New York: Columbia University Press, 2000).

Van Lennep, W., et al. (eds). *The London Stage 1660–1800* (Carbondale, IL: Southern Illinois University Press, 1968).

Ward, Colin. *Talking Schools* (London: Freedom Press, 1995).

Wollstonecraft, Mary. *Collected Letters of Mary Wollstonecraft*, edited by Ralph M. Wardle (Ithaca, NY: Cornell University Press, 1979).

Woodcock, George. *William Godwin: A Biographical Study* (London: Porcupine Press, 1946).

Index

The Pluto Press Newsletter

Hello friend of Pluto!

Want to stay on top of the best radical books
we publish?

Then sign up to be the first to hear about our
new books, as well as special events,
podcasts and videos.

You'll also get 50% off your first order with us
when you sign up.

Come and join us!

Go to bit.ly/PlutoNewsletter